East Keswick Millennium Book

East Keswick Millennium Book

A thousand year history of a Domesday Book village

East Keswick Millennium Group

© 2000

East Keswick Millennium Book

Written and published by the East Keswick Millennium Group

ISBN 0-9538815-0-4

© Copyright East Keswick Millennium Group 2000

The moral rights of the authors have been asserted.

All rights reserved

East Keswick Millennium Group

Secretary: A J Batty, 6 Keswick Grange, East Keswick LS17 9BX

mail@eastkeswick.org.uk

www.eastkeswick.org.uk

Printed in England

Designed and typeset by Creative Marketing Services

Editor
Andrew Batty

Writers & Researchers
Colin Asher
Andrew Batty
Joyce Evans
Bruce Jagger
Liz Parr

Additional Research
Shirley Doyle
Margaret Moseley
John Simpson
Melanie Smith

East Keswick Millennium Group Management
Victor Watson CBE (Chairman)
Andrew Batty (Secretary)
Duncan Pidsley (Treasurer)
Erica Smith (Advertising and Sponsorship)
Shirley Doyle
Jan Dower
Bruce Jagger
Liz Parr
Melanie Smith
Pat Stodart

The writers and researchers would particularly like to acknowledge the assistance given by the librarians and archivists of Leeds City Libraries, West Yorkshire Archives at Sheepscar and Wakefield, Yorkshire Archaeological Society, the Borthwick Institute at the University of York, the Brotherton collection of the University of Leeds, the Museum of the History of Education at the University of Leeds and numerous villagers including Mrs F Brierley, Mrs J Gallant and the East Keswick Parish Council, Derek Illingworth, Pam Prior, Ron Sudderdean, Joan Waide and Anne Wragg

State of the

art printing at

both ends of

this century

WADDINGTON CHORLEYS LTD
world class innovation in graphics communication and direct marketing products
Manston Lane · Cross Gates · Leeds LS15 8AH · Telephone: 0113 225 5000 · Facsimile: 0113 225 5400 (General)
0113 225 5401 (Direct Mail) · 0113 225 5402 (Confidential) · Internet: www.chorleys.co.uk · eMail: crossgates@chorleys.co.uk
London Office: 8 John Street · London WC1N 2ES · Telephone: 0171 269 7770 · Facsimile: 0171 269 7779 · eMail: london@chorleys.co.uk

The East Keswick Millennium Book could not have been possible without the generous financial support of a wide number of individuals and organisations. These included

The Scarman Trust and the Yorkshire Post Newspapers backed 'Can Do' initiative

Peter Asquith

WOOD HALL
HOTEL, HEALTH AND LEISURE CLUB

a million miles from anywhere...
...yet only minutes from the city.

Trip Lane, Linton,
West Yorkshire LS22 4JA
Tel: 01937 587271
Fax: 01937 584353
Email: events.woodhall@arcadianhotels.co.uk
www.arcadianhotels.co.uk

From jogging tracks, to badger watching, to woodland paint-ball, to safari archery, to eastern therapies, to days of luxury, to wedding ceremonies, to anniversaries, to an evening of music, to afternoon tea... think of Wood Hall.

Part of East Keswick's Heritage

R. ILLINGWORTH LTD.

Butchers of Distinction

Main Street, East Keswick
☎ 10937 572815
Email: philip@illingworthbutchers.fsnet.co.uk

BREWIN DOLPHIN
Local knowledge, national expertise

Personal investment advice
Corporate finance
Pension fund management & SIPPs
Charities & trust fund management

for further information contact:
Richard Wilkinson
34 Lisbon Street, Leeds LS1 4LX
Tel 0113 241 0158. Fax 0113 241 0111
web: www.brewindolphin.co.uk
email: info@brewin.co.uk

A division of

BREWIN DOLPHIN SECURITIES LTD
Incorporating
BREWIN DOLPHIN • BELL LAWRIEWHITE • WISE SPEKE
A member of the London Stock Exchange
and regulated by The Securities and Futures Authority Limited

Patrons

The East Keswick Millennium Group will always be indebted to the following villagers who had the confidence in the project and the team to donate towards making the idea a reality.

Alyson Ballman
Mr & Mrs Stubbs
Richard & Sarah Watson
Mr & Mrs Illingworth
Arthur Marshall
Shelagh Day
Allen Day
Victor & Sheila Watson
David Lupton
Susan Lupton
Dr Christopher & Mrs Wendy Watson
Peter Watson
In Memoriam:
    Gillian (Gilly) Watson 1971-1993
Peter & Wendy Wray
Doris Crowther
Robin Clark
Eleanor Jane Cooper
Steve & Kate Holliday
Miss Charlotte E Mackie
Mrs A J Kellet
The Priestley Family
Gill & Bobby Hinchliffe
John W Eaton BEng CEng MIEE
Robert G Illingworth, John D Illingworth & Kay C Illingworth/Jones
Margaret Anne Fairley

Ken Gale
Sandra Gardiner
Mrs Carol Brown
Kimberly Margaret Dee
Nicholas Paul James Dee
Jane & Allan Beardsworth
Josephine Alice Mather-Hunter
Paul Winter
Judith Bentley
Anthony & Simone Marcus
Georgina Ravenscroft
Patrick Henry
Michael Bartlett
D & E Loncraine
East Keswick Parish Council

Other donations were received from
Barclays Bank plc (Roger Browne)
David & Melanie Smith
Mr & Mrs J M Thornton
Mr Hanen
Sylvia Pinkney
Eddie & Elizabeth Tinsley
Peter Gallant
Mrs F M Watson

ADDLESHAW BOOTH & CO

Law Firm of the Year

Addleshaw Booth & Co is delighted to support East Keswick, the Millennium Village

To sample our nationally recognised expertise, contact either Paul Lee, Senior Partner or Mark Jones, Managing Partner

www.addleshaw-booth.co.uk

THE LAWYER
LAW FIRM OF THE YEAR

Sovereign House
PO Box 8
Sovereign Street
Leeds LS1 1HQ
Tel 0113 209 2000
Fax 0113 209 2000

100 Barbirolli Square
Manchester
M2 3AB
Tel 0161 934 6000
Fax 0161 934 6060

60 Cannon Street
London
EC4N 6NP
Tel 020 7982 5000
Fax 020 7982 5060

The Duke of Wellington

Family run pub by
Jayne, Nick Burrell and children

Modern and contemporary cooking at
The Blue Room

Telephone: 01937 573259

BROADCAST NEWS

- Video/CD Rom production
- Media Training
- Video News Releases
- Broadcast Counsultancy

Work with Professional
Broadcast Journalists

Contact Erica Smith on:
01937 572343
Email us on: bcast.news@ndirect.co.uk

Bush House, Brooklands, East Keswick,
Leeds LS17 9DD

Contents

	Patrons	ix
	Preface	xiii
	Foreword by Lord Harewood	xvii
	Introduction	xix
1	The first five hundred years	1
2	Tudor and Stuart days	13
3	Land ownership 1739-1951: the Lascelles factor	25
4	Farming in the Eighteenth Century	37
5	The Enclosure Act changes all	49
6	Farms, smallholdings and nurseries	59
7	Religion	79
8	East Keswick schools and schooldays - Education for all 1815-1914	87
9	The Village School: A century of change, 1914-1990	103
10	Transport & turnpikes	121
11	Notable houses	129
12	The village expands	147
13	Wildlife Trust	177
14	A vibrant social scene	183
15	The final night of a thousand years	195

Smith Devenish

Commercial Property
Development
and Investment

Meadow House, East Keswick

Preface

In the summer of 1998, with the millennium only eighteen months distant, many communities across the world started to consider how to mark this epoch in a befitting way.

In East Keswick, the Parish Council appealed for ideas and a public meeting was called to discuss the contenders.

There had been two previous booklets about the village published by the Women's Institute, but no larger scale book had ever been produced. Andrew Batty proposed that this be corrected and that a book be attempted to begin from the year 1000AD and to progress all the way through to Millennium Eve 1999. It was an ambitious project but one which won overwhelming support. A Millennium Group was properly constituted under the chairmanship of Victor Watson and a significant number of villagers were eager to help in any way they could.

One way was through involvement in the Millennium Group's second project. For apart from this book, a millennium gala weekend was planned for midsummer 2000, and so it came about that during three scorching summer days in June the village was treated to a flower festival, traditional village gala, barn dance and musical concert.

This book was, however, much the most ambitious project financially, and raising the funds to make this enterprise possible was a major task. The group approached a significant number of charitable trusts, potential advertisers and appealed for patrons.

The fundraising effort got off to a flying start with a reception on the terrace of Harewood House. Erica Smith who had volunteered to take on the task of advertising, sponsorship and donations proved a major asset to the team and a significant stage was reached when Andrew Batty made a successful presentation to the Scarman Trust which resulted in a £2000 grant.

This grant was backed by the *Yorkshire Evening Post* as part of their 'Can Do' initative and the newspaper - together with *Wetherby News* - gave valuable publicity to our efforts. Every press mention was followed by mail from across the UK; some from former villagers, others from those with affectionate childhood memories of the village from camping trips or Sunday School outings.

Finally, in mid 2000, with the book almost written, the Countryside Agency completed

125 years old and still in **great shape** for the new Millennium!

The Millennium has seen Leeds & Holbeck Building Society reach a landmark 125 years of continuous quality service to the people of Yorkshire.

Looking forward to the next 125 years of mutuality, we remain dedicated to the needs of our members, taking care of you – not shareholders.

As one of the top 10 building societies, with over 60 branches, Leeds & Holbeck still provides the kind of personal service that existed back in the early days.

And, with 20 branches in the Leeds area alone, you really don't have to go very far to enjoy the great range of products available.

LEEDS & HOLBECK BUILDING SOCIETY

It **pays** to belong

Head Office: 105 Albion Street, Leeds LS1 5AS
www.leeds-holbeck.co.uk

our fund raising efforts with a grant exceeding five thousand pounds. Their support was the catalyst behind the evolution of the writing team into a local history group which aimed to continue uncovering the area's rich heritage in the following years.

For the previous two years the small volunteer writing group had invested vast amounts of their own free time checking archive information, speaking to people with first hand memories and finding the missing pieces of a jigsaw of historical data.

Colin Asher was our writer responsible for the education sections of our book. Joyce Evans toiled over deeds, tithes and wrote the chapters on farming and land ownership. Bruce Jagger took on religion and notable houses, whilst Liz Parr covered the difficult to research early centuries. Andrew Batty compiled the remaining chapters on transport, village expansion and the closing years of the twentieth century. Of course this is a very simplistic summary of each core-writer's involvement. In truth, almost everyone had some involvement in each chapter. Two years on and sixty thousand words later, this is the result. We hope you enjoy it.

Andrew Batty
October 2000

timeless
24 hour banking by telephone or internet

what's next...
firstdirect.com
0800 24 24 24

Accounts opened subject to status. To maintain a quality service, calls may be monitored and/or recorded. First Direct is a division of HSBC Bank plc.

Foreword

By the Earl of Harewood

I have always been fascinated by history - glamorous, hard-to-envisage events like the Armada or the Field of the Cloth of Gold or the Crusades, as well as more readily approached affairs like Wellington's campaigns or the Treaty of Versailles. One of my earliest enthusiasms was for John Jones's *History of Harewood*, published in 1859 with, of course, an entry for East Keswick and incidentally several members of the village on the subscription list.

What better way then of celebrating the Millennium than embarking on an in-depth study of a place and a community, admittedly not vast but of real local significance. The past axiomatically sheds light on the present and future, and the uncovering of events and personalities is not only fascinating because of the detail but invaluable in itself. History after all is not just about earth-shaking upheavals but about the not-so-ordinary men and women who caused the changes and perhaps suffered as a result of them. Us in fact.

Significant names and occurrences are thrown up as these pages chronicle local history, like the Gascoignes of Gawthorpe who produced the most famous of any mediaeval Lord Chief Justice, or the Earl of Strafford, whose support of Charles I did not save him from execution. Some readers (like me) will be amazed to read that Scottish raiders in the time of English King Edward II penetrated so far south as to be responsible for sacking Harewood Church in 1316, though maybe, as the book suggests, they and the Danes before them missed East Keswick, much as centuries later German bombers almost invariably failed to locate either Leeds or its Northern satellites because, I have always understood, of fortuitous cloud formations on the nights which were suitable for bombing excursions.

Early on, an influence on East Keswick is described quite simply (and not inaccurately) as '1739-1951: The Lascelles Factor'. Indeed, my family has had East Keswick connections ever since they moved from the North Riding to Harewood in 1739, and they were only ended, somewhat involuntarily, in 1951 with the last of the sales forced on us by death duties of some 70% after my father died in 1947. My own part in this history, apart from concern with these sales, is fairly slight - attendance at the closure of the school, membership of the Harewood cricket team which pre-1939 regularly played East Keswick, and as donor in 1948 of the site of the village hall. Personal memories are also sporadic but fairly positive. My brother and I regularly rode before the war as far as the western edge of East Keswick, and we more than once attended meets of the Bramham Moor hounds in the village. In addition, we used to go to the late night carol services in the church at Christmas time. There wasn't one at Harewood Church.

The account of East Keswick school provides one of the book's most entertaining chapters and incidentally introduced me to a new word when poor attendance in October 1917 is put down to absence for 'potato scratting'. I cringed as the Diocesan Inspector a year or so later opined that 'it would be well if the children were able to apply the lessons of Holy Scripture to their lives more fully' but rejoiced that some years further on he (or his successor) was able to praise the 'spirit of tranquillity' which pervaded the school, though wondering if the school mistress, Miss Helm - a heroine by all accounts and regularly triumphant over adversity - would in this phrase have recognised the community over which she presided. The story is full of convincing incident, though with the school's ultimate closure it inevitably makes slightly melancholy reading.

This chronicle sets out to be a modern Domesday Book, and whilst reading it, I became convinced that it fully lived up to Archbishop Wulfstan's rubric which adorns the first chapter. More than that you can't ask.

The Rt Hon the Earl of Harewood KBE

September 2000

Introduction

The landscape

Just over 300 million years ago what is now Yorkshire was just south of the equator. Sandstones, including the tough millstone grit used in the construction of many Victorian buildings in West Yorkshire, originated from this period. Some 80 million years later the same area had moved a few degrees further north and the magnesium limestone, which now forms a ridge roughly following the course of the today's A1 trunk road, emerged from a dried-up seabed. The land that is now East Keswick arrived at its current latitude within the last 50 million years. The east of the village rests right on the edge of the magnesium limestone ridge while to the west there is sandstone with outcrops of millstone grit. Deposits of sand, gravel and clay were left behind by the Ice Age some 10,000 years ago.

On the eve of the last millennium local inhabitants looking south towards Bardsey and Wike or north across the Wharfe valley would have seen a landscape that we would probably recognise in the twenty-first century. There had already been extensive clearance of woodland and nearly a third of the land in the village may have been cultivated. Over the last thousand years the familiar contours have provided the backcloth for a changing pattern of fields, buildings and highways, but the boundaries of the early settlement appear to have been much the same as those of the modern civil parish.

Today East Keswick has eight and half miles of boundary between the River Wharfe and

Keswick Beck. In the northwest corner is an area called Keswick Fitts (meaning river meadow), which may have been added to the settlement following changes in the course of the river. The boundary continues eastwards with the Wharfe past Ox Close. On the other side of the river is the Parish of Sicklinghall and early maps show a ford near the site of today's iron bridge. From the edge of Collingham the village boundary leaves the river through what is now a residential area before following Harewood Road east for just over one hundred yards. Turning south there are the remains of a wide hedge that in the Middle Ages divided Collingham's West Field from East Keswick's Beck Field. The hedge then thins out and is obviously less mature in the vicinity of the old railway. Views of this eastern boundary where Keswick Beck flows towards Collingham can still be enjoyed from the end of School Lane.

The Beck is a shallow stream which would never have formed too much of an impediment to the movement of people and livestock, but nevertheless it has maintained the boundary with Bardsey for over a thousand years. On the left of the road entering the village from Bardsey and Wike, a row of mature waterside trees marks the boundary. Upstream, near to Burns Farm, the watercourse was diverted to the north at some time during the eighteenth century but East Keswick did not give up the few metres of land and boundary stones were erected to show the original demarcation.

From Burns Farm to Harewood Avenue the original boundary seems to have followed a small stream, suggested by the contours but no longer in evidence. On a 1690s Harewood Estate map this formed the division between Harewood Common and East Keswick Moor and was labelled 'Fletcher Dyke Dry in Somer'. From this westerly point, marked as Gallow Hill on the same map, the boundary runs east across pasture before descending along field boundaries to Keswick Fitts.

The Settlement

The earliest date of human occupation within these boundaries is not known. The Sites and Monuments Record of the West Yorkshire Archaeological Service lists a number of cropmarks discernable from aerial photographs which may suggest early settlements. A few miles away, Wetherby had a Roman settlement and there are remains of a Roman villa at Collingham. Roman pottery has also been found at Wike but all that is known about East Keswick is that, some time before the eleventh century, isolated farms had come together to form a settlement between the Wharfe and Keswick Beck. The earliest recorded name for East Keswick was Chesinc or Chesuic, thought to have derived from an Old English word for cheese or dairy farm. This settlement was a single agricultural

The landscape has changed little over the last thousand years. This beautiful vista of the Wharfe Valley is taken from the end of Cleavesty Lane and shown on a 1930s postcard entitled Surprise View. It is still known as that today.

unit forming part of a larger Anglo Saxon estate based on Harewood. The same estate appears to have been the basis for the early ecclesiastical Parish of Harewood of which East Keswick was a part.

Following Viking invasions, counties had been divided into administrative districts called wapentakes, where weapons could be counted and taxes levied. Settlements at East Keswick, Harewood, Bardsey and Collingham were all separate vills or townships in the north-eastern corner of the Wapentake of Skyrack. Skyrack included settlements lying between the Rivers Aire and Wharfe, from beyond Ilkley Moor in the west, and eastwards to a line approximately following the route of the A1 between these two rivers. The administrative centre was the shire oak at Headingley where assemblies would be held by the shire reeve or sheriff. The community formed in East Keswick before the end of the first millennium has had a continuous history to the present day.

1

The first five hundred years

The new millennium

And then there is also a need
that each should understand
where he came from and what he is -
and what will become of him.

(Wulfstan, Archbishop of York 1002-1023)

If the date of our new millennium has given rise to some controversy, the first day of January in the year one thousand probably passed with little comment in East Keswick. Many people would in any case have been unaware of the date and, according to the old style calendar, a new year started on Lady Day (25th March). However, those who were familiar with the scriptures would have been aware that the Book of Revelation spoke of the devil being let loose in the world after a thousand years. Some were prepared to see impending doom in natural phenomena like the brilliant star in 989 that became known as Halley's comet. Others interpreted the misery inflicted by the Vikings as a sign of God's wrath. One such was Archbishop Wulfstan of York who sometimes used the pen name Lupus or 'wolf'. The *Sermon of the Wolf*, written fourteen years into the new millennium, gave dire warnings about the state of society one thousand years after the birth of Christ. Wulfstan claimed the Vikings were acting as instruments of the Anti-Christ and he would have intended that his words should be relayed to the public by monks and parish priests. At a time when few people could read or write, the pulpit was an important way of spreading ideas. We do not know whether the sermon was ever delivered in East Keswick. There was no church there and, in the absence of a visiting preacher, it would have been necessary to cross the fields to Harewood, joining parishioners from neighbouring settlements of Newall, Stockton, Lofthouse and Stubhouse (all now part of Harewood) and from the villages of Dunkeswick, Weeton, Weardley and Wike.

There are very few records of West Yorkshire in the early eleventh century and none relating to East Keswick. With the help of evidence from other areas, however, we can build a picture of a small community living around the present day Main Street and Moor Lane area. Small houses or huts were constructed from a wooden frame stuck into the ground and covered with wattle and daub, which was a mixture of clay, straw and dung. Peasants' cottages usually comprised a single living area with a hearth divided from another smaller chamber for sleeping. The roof was thatched and there were no windows. Although the buildings, like their occupants, belonged to the landlord, most families probably kept some livestock of their own and almost certainly cultivated their own vegetables. Parsnips, carrots, onions, leeks, cabbages and several herbs could be grown and these probably formed the basis of their diet, supplemented by mutton and pork when available. (Spinach, sprouts, cauliflower, runner beans and potatoes had yet to be introduced.) The hedgerows and woods supplemented their meals but there were no rabbits until after the Norman Conquest.

We can imagine the rich farmyard smells, the mud, the lack of privacy and the disease. Life was controlled by the seasons and involved much hard physical labour. (By contrast, monasteries offered, in addition, education and contemplation while in towns there were opportunities for trade.) These were undoubtedly hard times. At certain seasons food stocks would run low and, more disastrously, there were years when crops failed, as recorded in 1000 and 1005. A more positive view of rural life can be derived from contemporary writings about estate management. Archbishop Wulfstan, referred to above, is thought to be the author of two such works. He discussed the rights and obligations of both landlord and serf. In particular, he outlined that the ploughman and his assistant belonged to the lord and their primary duty was to work for no pay on his land in return for his protection. They could also earn payment in kind by ploughing land belonging to others. Wulfstan suggested that the mutual dependence resulting from the requirements of the agricultural estate would help to maintain a happy community, but landlords were urged to be sensitive to local customs and to organise appropriate rewards and concessions in the interests of good working relationships. Celebrations after spring ploughing, haymaking and harvest were the high points of the year. Landlords were encouraged to provide generous amounts of food, to be washed down with mead, a strong alcoholic drink based on honey.

The Domesday Survey and the aftermath of the Norman Conquest

A blue plaque on Stocks Hill commemorates the fact that East Keswick was mentioned in the Domesday Book based on a survey of 1086. The settlement was designated a manor, a term which described a single agricultural estate. The amount of land recorded for taxation purposes was five *carucates*. This could have represented anything from five to nine hundred acres under cultivation. The survey gives no indication of the number of inhabitants looking after this land but there were three ploughs which typically would have needed teams of eight oxen each. It was recorded that before the Norman Conquest this manor called Chesinc was in the hands of the Saxon lord Tor, who was also listed as one of three lords of Harewood.

After 1066 William the Conqueror had taken control of large parts of the North of England in a series of raids that became known as the 'harrying of the North'. He used some of these lands to reward Norman families who had helped to secure his succession. Harewood, along with the townships of East Keswick, Alwoodley, Weardley, Wigton, Wike, Dunkeswick and Weeton, were granted to a knight called Robert de Romilly in return for his continued military support. This gift also included extensive estates around Skipton where the family were based, and early in the twelfth century his daughter Cecily endowed an Augustinian monastery nearby at Embsay. Later the monks moved to Bolton Priory on the banks of the Wharfe and income from the de Romilly estates, including Harewood, contributed to their upkeep.

Around the year 1135 Cecily's son Ranulf died and the vast estates were divided between his two married sisters. Avice de Romilly and her husband William de Curci succeeded to Harewood and they confirmed that the church there, as well as the farms and mills in the surrounding townships, would continue to pay rents to Bolton Priory. This connection between Harewood and Bolton was to continue until Henry VIII broke up the monastic estates in the sixteenth century.

Under the feudal system the ownership of land was based on a hierarchy of military service owed to the King. In the same way that the King shared out land among his friends, so the feudal lords could lease parts of their estates to people who had served them. Again there would be an obligation to provide military service, although later this was replaced by a monetary payment. By 1166 a Simon de Mohaut, whose family may have served under de Romilly at the Conquest, had been granted eight *caracutes* of land in East Keswick and part of Wike in return for half a Knight's Fee (military service) to the lords of Harewood. Three or four generations of the family (variously spelt as de Montealto, Maude, etc) held the manor of East Keswick until about 1280.

The Moated Site and The Manor of East Keswick

The de Mohauts had been given other estates near Keighley and Bingley and it is not known whether they spent much time in East Keswick. However, it may have been the last Simon de Mohaut who built the moated hall that occupied a site south of the present day Moat House in Moor Lane.

Although known locally as Gascoigne's Castle, it is not clear what connection the hall had with that family. It resembles the sites of other thirteenth century manor houses in Yorkshire, comprising a raised rectangular platform surrounded by a flat-bottomed ditch. Typically these sites extended to about one acre and were built to take advantage of nearby springs. In this case there was another embankment on the south side because of the sloping ground. The house itself was less than one hundred feet square and was situated at the northern end of the platform where a causeway crossed the moat. Stone from the abandoned house is said to have been used to build Old Hall Farm and Moat House in the eighteenth century but the original construction could have been timber.

Such residences were usually built by the local lord as a sign of prestige rather than defence. Although their construction did give a measure of security, it is unlikely that this site would have withstood determined efforts of bands of Scots in one of their forays into the North of England. Moated houses were relatively cheap to build compared with the castles aspired to by the richer and more important feudal lords, but they did rely on the availability of a sufficient labour force which was more likely to have existed before the Black Death in the mid fourteenth century. Most sites of this type were constructed between 1250 and 1325 when the exploitation of small estates by minor lords was at its peak. Many were completed before 1275, which would be consistent with the assumption that the third Simon de Mohaut, who died around 1280, built East Keswick's manor house.

The site was bulldozed in 1960 but there still stands nearby an ancient oak, thought to be 600 years old and the oldest tree in East Keswick, which would have shared the landscape with the moated house.

After the death of the last Simon de Mohaut the manor passed to his seven married daughters. There is a record that in 1299 the inheritance of one of these daughters, Elizabeth Langfield, was given to her nephew William de Ilketon. She was to retain a life interest in return for 'a yearly rent of a rose at Midsummer and doing services to the chief lord ....' In 1316 this William de Ilketon was one of three men named as 'lords' of the vill in a survey called *Nomina Villarum*. The others, Brian de Thornhill and Peter de Martheley had also acquired their interest in the manor of East Keswick directly from other de Mohaut heiresses. We can only speculate that Brian de Thornhill may have occupied the moated house for a time. He was the only one of these three lords to be named in the Lay Subsidy (a tax raised on the value of moveable goods) levied in 1327. His name appears first in a list of the six East Keswick residents assessed as liable for the tax. In 1372 John de Ilketon sold his share of the manor of East Keswick to John Fairfax and Roger Lythum but from this date there are no records of the manor until the early sixteenth century when it reappears in connection with a branch of the Gascoigne family.

The rise of the Gascoignes

In the late thirteenth century a William Gascoigne had married the heiress of John of Gawthorpe, a freeman farming in Harewood. From this point the fortunes of the family rose. Each heir was named William and there are thought to have been eleven or twelve generations of this branch of the family before the male line died out in 1587. Originally in the shadow of the neighbouring lords of Harewood, the ambitious Gascoigne family eventually built a large house near where Harewood House now stands. In 1480 the eighth William Gascoigne was granted a licence to fortify his house and enclose part of his lands in Harewood and surrounding villages.

As early as 1370 the family had been accepted as members of the lesser gentry. The famous Lord Chief Justice Gascoigne (1350 - 1419) and his heirs continued the process of building up an estate that rivalled Harewood itself. No contemporary references have been found to a Gascoigne living in East Keswick although it is possible that the name 'Gascoigne's Castle' came about because a branch of the family lived in the moated house during the fifteenth century. (Later a Thomas Gascoigne lived in the village in the 1620s but nothing else is known about him apart from the fact that he had three daughters.)

East Keswick

Monasteries and mills

The few sources for the history of this period include documents called 'feet of fines' which established who owned land. However, these, like the records of the monastic houses, portray life from a landlord's point of view and there is scant information about the lives of ordinary people. In 1166 Affric de Keswick, who was probably a tenant farmer, witnessed the confirmation of a grant of some twenty acres of land by Simon de Mohaut to Pontefract Priory. Twenty years later his son exchanged this land for a different twenty acres elsewhere in the village. Land may also have been given to Sinningthwaite Priory, a Cistercian nunnery near Thorp Arch, and in 1203 Henry, son of Jordan, granted land in East Keswick to Fountains Abbey. Donations to religious houses were common in the twelfth and thirteenth centuries. Not only did the monasteries play an important role in the economy of the region, but such gestures by local lords may also have conferred some status on their families at a time when religion played an important part in the life of the whole population. In rural communities, where literacy was rare, Christian teaching mixed with superstition conspired to keep villagers in awe of priests and monks.

As we have seen, through the overlordship of Harewood, East Keswick maintained its links with Bolton Priory. The monastic estates were mostly further north in Wharfedale, where the main source of income was the sale of wool. Rents from the arable land lower down the valley contributed to their prosperity. In 1285 the heirs of Simon de Mohaut were required do the 'accustomed services' in return for the land they held from the canon of Bolton Priory. Their customary tenants in Harewood owed the monastery twenty-two days service each year and the same may have applied in East Keswick.

Another source of monastic income came from mills. The account books of Bolton Priory record rents from a mill at East Keswick between 1286 and 1325. In 1304, for example, there was an income of thirteen shillings and four pence. In the same year a mill at Alwoodley yielded only five shillings while Harewood, with at least two mills, paid twenty-two pounds. In some places income was boosted by forcing all the inhabitants to make use of their local mill rather than doing the grinding at home. Early in the fourteenth century the economic fortunes of the monastery declined significantly and it is not known how long the mill survived in East Keswick or even where it was situated. A possible site is near the present day footbridge over Keswick Beck at the southern entrance to the village. The area of the marsh across the road has the appearance of a silted up millpond and the route of the road over the beck could have been the site of the milldam. Mediaeval mills did not require large quantities of water and other mills in West Yorkshire occupied similar positions where a stream formed the boundary with a neighbouring settlement. However, a mill on the River Wharfe is also a possibility. Near the present day iron bridge there is some stonework which may suggest a post-mediaeval mill, and the first Ordnance Survey map refers to Millgate Quarry at the end of Crabtree Lane. An even earlier reference to 'Mylnegate' has been recorded in 1316 but there is no evidence of its location.

Legal matters

At the point where the boundaries of Harewood, Bardsey and East Keswick meet was an area of common. Landowners and tenants had grazing rights in that part which belonged to their own settlement, but there appear to have been few physical barriers to make these divisions clear. In 1209 the lords of Harewood had hundreds of sheep on the common and the Abbot of Kirkstall, who owned the manor of Bardsey, found it necessary to describe in court all the ditches and streams between Wike and Keswick Beck which formed the abbey land's western boundary

There were further disputes. In the vicinity of present day Burns Farm an area of common pasture known as Langwood was used for grazing cattle. John de Medelton, a tenant farmer from East Keswick, had complained that he had been deprived of his rights there. He cited not only the monks and lay brothers of Kirkstall but also others from around Harewood who had grazed their cattle on the common. However in 1284 records of the York Assizes state that

> The Abbat says that the place called Langwode is not in the vill of Estkesewyk, but is in Berdesey. The jury say that Langwode is in Berdesey, and so the writ fails.

The following year the Countess of Albermarle of Harewood complained that the Kirkstall monks had impounded '8 cows and 4 bullocks from Harewode in a place called Langewode'. It may be that there was a shortage of grazing land for, after the death of the third Simon de Mohaut, his heirs also apparently ran into problems with the vigilant monks who denied them access to common pasture they claimed was in Bardsey.

An original deed dated 12th May 1301 in the Yorkshire Archaeological Society Archives describes the right of one Adam de Middleton to receive three quarters of corn each year from Elizabeth de Mohaut. It is not clear whether he was connected with the John de Medelton who complained of being deprived of his rights on the common at Langwood or whether he actually lived in East Keswick. However, it was found necessary to establish that, when Elizabeth's property in East Keswick reverted to

William de Ilketon on her death, he was also to be bound by the agreement to pay the same quantity of corn during Adam's lifetime. Adam was granted 'power to distrain from all his tenements in the vill of Kesewik if the corn were in arrear.' Other records show that William de Ilketon needed to be persuaded to pay his debts. In 1322 he owed a John Bush one hundred and three shillings and ten years later he and his son Nicholas owed eighteen pounds to a John de Neusam.

Plague and Conflict

Between 1315 and 1320 a series of bad harvests and torrential rains affected not only Yorkshire but also the whole of Europe. There was disease among sheep and cattle and the price of food rose sharply. Village life must have become more difficult. The feudal ties that bound the serfs to the lords were beginning to be loosened. There was less unpaid labour on the lord's own land, but a rise in population had put pressure on rural communities. In East Keswick the majority of the inhabitants were labourers, still living in very basic housing. After Robert the Bruce's victory at Bannockburn in 1314 there were frequent raids in the North of England. In 1316, a year of famine, exceptional rainfall and cold weather, the Scots sacked Harewood Church and they returned to the area two years later. Between 1320 and 1325 Bolton Priory spent over ninety pounds repairing Harewood mill and dam, expenditure that is likely to have resulted from the damage inflicted by the Scots. East Keswick residents could not have been unaware of this destruction and some may well have been involved in skirmishes, but it would be good to think that the sheltered settlement down by Keswick Beck escaped the notice of the aggressive Scots as they rampaged through Yorkshire.

As well as encouraging the Scots to cross into northern counties, the incompetence of Edward II, who reigned from 1307 - 1327, led to unrest among his barons. In revenge for the death of one of his favourites, Edward sent his troops in pursuit of his cousin the Earl of Lancaster. In March 1322 Lancaster's army was retreating northwards and crossed the Wharfe at Wetherby. A few days later they were defeated at Boroughbridge by the King's supporters. Robert de Lisle, Lord of Harewood, fought on the King's side and was subsequently granted the King's protection for all his manors and towns including East Keswick.

As the fourteenth century entered its fourth decade there may have been some respite from the tribulations of the previous twenty years. 1332 was reported to be a year of excellent harvests and prosperity in the countryside. However, the relief was short-lived. In the 1340s there was more famine and in 1349 the Black Death reached Yorkshire. Rural economies were already in a bad way and this marked a low point. Further outbreaks of the plague occurred in 1361 and it has been estimated that up to fifty percent of the population of the north of England was wiped out in these epidemics.

The end of the Middle Ages

The plague was one reason why some mediaeval villages were abandoned but fortunately this was not the case with East Keswick. While we have no local records from that time, nationally the effect of the shortage of labour was to change the way the old mediaeval estates were run. More land was leased to tenants who would then employ wage labourers. Inevitably wages had to increase and because of this there was an incentive for landowners to reduce the amount of land in cultivation and convert to pasture if possible.

Records have been published for the 1379 Poll Tax in Skyrack. These provide some idea of the status of villagers and comparisons with neighbouring settlements. Taxes were levied according to wealth, with farm labourers paying the lowest assessment of four pence. Everyone aged fourteen or over except for beggars was supposed to be taxed.

The names of Thornhill and de Ilketon formerly linked with the manor appear in another document a year earlier but were apparently not resident in East Keswick in 1379. Instead, a Robert de Ecglislay heads the list of Poll Tax payers. He was described as a franklin (usually the farm bailiff). He paid three shillings and four pence while everyone else paid only four pence. Forty-five adults were taxed, suggesting a total population in the region of seventy. There would have been little chance to recover from the effects of the Black Death and it is likely that at the beginning of the century this figure would have been considerably higher.

There are obvious differences between East Keswick and Harewood. The former was a modest farming community while Harewood supported several tradesmen. According to the Poll Tax records, Harewood had two butchers, a draper, a hosteller and a shoemaker. But again the majority of the inhabitants paid the basic four pence. The mediaeval borough of Harewood seems to have been established near the modern village centre and south east of the original settlement near the Church. There had been a Saturday market and an annual July fair since 1208. William de Aldeburgh, who had become lord of the manor in 1364, heads the Poll Tax returns for Harewood. He had

1379 Poll Tax returns for Harewood and East Keswick

WAPPENTAGIUM DE SKYRAK'.

HARWOD'.

Willelmus de Aldeburgh', Chiualer,	xx.s.
Willelmus filius ejusdem Willelmi, Esquier,	iij.s. iiij.d.
Willelmus Prestmañ, Bocher, & vx	xij.d.
Thomas Serlsoñ, Draper, & vx	xij.d.
Willelmus Marschall', Hostiler, & vx	xij.d.
Robertus Prestmañ, Bocher, & vx	xij.d.
Hugo Louell', ffranklañ, & vx	iij.s. iiij.d.
Robertus fflynt, Sutor, & vx	vj.d.

(Membrane 42, column 2.)

Willelmus de Harwod' & vx	iiij.d.
Nicholaus Dansoñ & vx	iiij.d.
Johannes Seriaunt & vx	iiij.d.
Robertus ffare & vx	iiij.d.
Nicholaus Gilsoñ & vx	iiij.d.
Willelmus Pye & vx	iiij.d.
Willelmus Bensoñ & vx	iiij.d.
Johannes Gascone & vx	iiij.d.
Johannes Serlsoñ & vx	iiij.d.
Willelmus Cowhird' & vx	iiij.d.
Willelmus Wilsoñ & vx	iiij.d.
Ricardus Beestoñ & vx	iiij.d.
Robertus Marschall' & vx	iiij.d.
Johannes fflynt & vx	iiij.d.
Thomas Tybsoñ & vx	iiij.d.
Johannes Scotte & vx	iiij.d.
Johannes de Bayldoñ & vx	iiij.d.
Johannes Buteler & vx	iiij.d.
Robertus ffawkes & vx	iiij.d.
Adam Carter & vx	iiij.d.
Johannes Gobet & vx	iiij.d.
Robertus de Tyndale & vx	iiij.d.
Robertus Collok & vx	iiij.d.
Johannes Asche & vx	iiij.d.
Robertus Belle & vx	iiij.d.
Adam de Milforth & vx	iiij.d.
Johannes Grayneson & vx	iiij.d.
Ricardus de Haltoñ & vx	iiij.d.
Ricardus del More & vx	iiij.d.
Ricardus Whitteknaue & vx	iiij.d.
Thomas ffyndyrne & vx	iiij.d.
Henricus filius Roberti & vx	iiij.d.
Thomas del More & vx	iiij.d.
Ricardus Walker & vx	iiij.d.

Thomas Clerk & vx	iiij.d.
Willelmus Chaumbirlañ & vx	iiij.d.
Robertus Boteler & vx	iiij.d.
Willelmus Porter & vx	iiij.d.
Johannes del Kychyn & vx	iiij.d.
Margeria Rixan	iiij.d.
Walterus Wilmañ	iiij.d.
Johannes de Belañd'	iiij.d.
Robertus fflynt	iiij.d.
Cecilia de Bryttsby	iiij.d.
Johannes Belle	iiij.d.
Willelmus Thomemañ	iiij.d.
Thomas Jonmañ	iiij.d.
Alicia seruiens Johannis	iiij.d.
Summa—xlvij.s. ij.d.	

ESTKESWYK'.

Robertus de Ecglislay, ffranklañ,	iij.s.
Johannes Alansoñ & vx	iiij.d.
Thomas filius Nicholai & vx	iiij.d.
Thomas filius Johannis Wryth & vx	iiij.d.
Johannes filius Willelmi & vx	iiij.d.
Johannes Seegher & vx	iiij.d.
Willelmus Goderhayle & vx	iiij.d.
Robertus Buteler & vx	iiij.d.
Willelmus Tasker & vx	iiij.d.
Rogerus Dernele & vx	iiij.d.
Symoñ de Bedall' & vx	iiij.d.
Willelmus Hopwod' & vx	iiij.d.
Johannes Caluerlay & vx	iiij.d.
Johannes Batemañ & vx	iiij.d.
Johannes Wryght & vx	iiij.d.
Adam Milner & vx	iiij.d.
Nicholaus Holdenmañ & vx	iiij.d.
Robertus Wryghtsoñ & vx	iiij.d.
Matilda Wryght	iiij.d.
Thomas filius Johannis	iiij.d.
Nicholaus Batemañ	iiij.d.
Robertus Caluerlay	iiij.d.
Elena Buteler	iiij.d.
Magota filia Roberti	iiij.d.
Nicholaus filius Henrici	iiij.d.
Petronilla Webster	iiij.d.
Robertus del Stede	iiij.d.
Emma Milner	iiij.d.
Summa—xij.s. iiij.d.	

1379 Poll Tax returns for Harewood and East Keswick extracted from the Yorkhsire Archaeological Journal, vol 6, 1881

nb: Willelmus de Harwod' & vx~ shows that he had a wife

built the castle there and may have tried to contain the ambitions of his neighbours, the Gascoignes.

There is no documentary evidence relating specifically to East Keswick from the fifteenth century. Politically it was an unstable time. The adult male members of many of Yorkshire's leading families were involved in fighting in France or in the domestic battles of the period but, although they may have tried to recruit foot soldiers from their estates, small rural communities would have found it difficult to spare men from their work on the land. Not far from East Keswick a battle took place at Bramham Moor in 1408. Henry Percy, Duke of Northumberland, who commanded a rebellion of northern earls, was killed there by a force of Yorkshiremen led by Sir Thomas Rokeby, the county sheriff.

After the death of William de Aldburgh in 1390 the Harewood estates had been divided between his two married sisters. Their two families, the Redmans and the Rythers, shared the manorial rights for nearly two hundred years. Nearby the son of Lord Chief Justice Gascoigne continued his father's acquisition of land in Yorkshire and he fought for the Duchy of Lancaster in France.

From the mid-fifteenth century the Wars of Roses divided the landed Yorkshire families but probably had little impact on the lives of the poor. There was a Lancastrian victory near Wakefield in 1460 and Yorkist revenge early the following year at Towton near Tadcaster. The latter was a particularly bloody battle fought in a snowstorm and stories about the fields turning red and rivers and streams being clogged with bodies must have spread throughout the county. William Gascoigne received a pardon for his Lancastrian sympathies in 1461, although he later married into the Percy family who served the Duchy of Lancaster. In the 1480s his son may have fought for Richard III at the Battle of Bosworth but, like most of the gentry, he was granted a royal pardon on the succession of Henry Tudor. The family continued to prosper. They had enclosed some of their land in Gawthorpe and other villages. By the end of the fifteenth century the Gascoignes had apparently acquired the manor of East Keswick but no mention of the village has been found in records relating to the Gascoigne family until the 1520s.

Despite the political upheaval, social conditions began to improve. East Keswick had survived as an agricultural community. Villagers who managed to grow surplus produce could take it to the market at Harewood and stay around for some ale and company. In East Keswick the moated house is the only known residence of any size dating from before 1500 and it seems that, although the farmland was valued, the settlement was too small to attract wealthier landowners to put down roots.

A note on sources

The *West Yorkshire Archaeological Survey to AD 1500*, edited by Faull and Moorhouse, provides an introduction to Yorkshire during this period and has many useful references. There are few early records of the life and people of East Keswick but most of those used here have been published by the Yorkshire Archaeological Society and the Thoresby Society. The Journals of both societies also have many useful articles. Other works include *The Year 1000* by Robert Lacey, *Bolton Priory* by Ian Kershaw, *The History and Antiquities of Harewood* by John Jones, *British Battlefields, the North,* by Philip Warner, *Lower Wharfedale* by Harry Speight, *Thorner, the Making of a Yorkshire Village* by Terence Brown, *Yorkshire Boundaries* by HE Jean le Patourel and others and *The Moated Sites of Yorkshire* also by HE Jean le Patourel. A survey of East Keswick's parish boundary is in the archives of the West Yorkshire Archaeological Society, and the library there has an unpublished thesis by JW Reddyhoff entitled *The Lords of Harewood and the Gascoignes of Gawthorpe*. The geological note in the introduction is based on a text prepared by Julia Morgan for the Wildlife Trust.

2

Tudor and Stuart days

Lords and manors

The history of manorial arrangements is complex and often confusing. In any event, after the Black Death the significance of the manor of East Keswick declined. At the beginning of the thirteenth century Simon de Mohaut had effectively owned the whole village but four hundred years later what remained of manorial rights was merely a source of rental income. References to the manor of East Keswick are found in records of land transactions involving various members of the Yorkshire gentry, none of whom ever lived in the village. One was Christopher de Warde, a member of a notable Guiseley family who had been a standard bearer for Henry III at the siege of Boulogne and who died in 1522. During his lifetime he had collected seven Yorkshire manors including that of East Keswick. The latter may have been a wedding gift at the time he married the daughter of Sir William Gascoigne of Gawthorpe.

Although the Gascoignes no longer held the manor of East Keswick, they did own some of the tenanted farms. The William Gascoigne who had succeeded in 1487 and lived until 1551 was a colourful figure. According to William Wentworth, who later inherited the Gawthorpe estate, he was 'reputedly more like a great earl than a knight' and he must have been a formidable figure to all local residents. He was at various times an MP, a Commissioner for collecting taxes and a Justice of the Peace. It is likely that it was he, rather than the Redmans and Rythers at Harewood Castle or the non-resident landlords of East Keswick, who was regarded by village people as the local squire. He became a leading member of the Yorkshire gentry but despite his status he had a volatile temperament and would often use force to get his own way.

A Riotous Knight

Because of his sometimes violent behaviour, Gascoigne had experience of the law from both sides, and in published records of the Star Chamber Proceedings there is an example of him leading local tenants and labourers in a riot. Three days before Christmas in 1529 two farmers from East Keswick, William Clough and William Smythe, joined Gascoigne and a crowd of at least fifty men from Harewood and surrounding villages. The complaint to the court names Gascoigne's two sons, several gentlemen, tenant farmers and local labourers who, 'together with dyuerse other rioutous persons', broke into the church armed with swords, staves and knives and assaulted Thomas Clarke, a chaplain.

Clarke was one of six chantry priests or chaplains provided by Bolton Priory for the private chapel of the lords of Harewood, which was based in the Parish Church. (It had been set up by the mid fourteenth century lord of Harewood, Robert de Lisle.) These priests probably assisted the vicars who otherwise had no help with the spiritual and pastoral responsibilities of a very widespread parish. The chaplains may also have organised a school for the children of the leading Harewood and Gawthorpe families.

Clarke reported that he feared for his life when threatened by this mob who

> with great violence and rigorous maner plucked your said orator out of the said church, and other great enormytees then and ther did to him.

It is not clear what he had done to deserve this frightening attack but three other chaplains apparently joined Gascoigne in the riot. Neither is it known what, if any, punishment was meted out for the offence. However, Thomas Clarke, though elderly, survived the ordeal and was still in post at the time of the Dissolution ten years later. The three chaplains who took part in the riot appear to have departed Harewood by then.

It was not the only time that Gascoigne took the law into his own hands but he was also able to round up local support for more legitimate reasons. A survey was conducted in 1539 to discover how many soldiers and weapons would be available to Henry VIII. In these records, known as Muster Rolls, Gascoigne had an impressive thirty men 'redy at all times to do the Kynge's service with horse and harness.' Among these thirty men was a William Clough who may have been the loyal tenant from East Keswick who was involved in the Harewood Church riot. (His name does not appear in the East Keswick Musters although he would probably still have been of fighting age.) In 1545 Gascoigne was required to raise men for a garrison on the Scottish Borders and it is possible that East Keswick residents were among the fifty men he sent.

The Reformation

By the Act of Supremacy in 1534 Henry VIII broke from the Church of Rome and thereafter set about acquiring for himself the wealth of the monastic estates in England. The Yorkshire abbeys and many of the long established landowning families were not prepared to accept the break with Rome without a fight. A protest known as the Pilgrimage of Grace was organised in 1536. Henry Ryther of Harewood Castle very reluctantly gave his support to the King's minister, Thomas Cromwell. Likewise Sir William Gascoigne paid lip service to the reforms. However, it has been suggested that, when required by the King to raise a force to assist Lord Darcy at Pontefract Castle, he gave his support to the Pilgrims. Darcy, of Temple Newsam near Leeds, had been ordered by the King to resist the rebels but his sympathies lay with them and he surrendered without a fight. As a result Darcy was executed but Gascoigne was pardoned. The latter may not actually have played a very active part in the rebellion. He was by then aged about sixty-eight and somewhat infirm. Two years earlier he had complained that he had 'a great defect of the emmerodes' and could not ride more than sixteen miles a day. (This excuse had been made when he had been arrested and was required to travel to London to answer charges arising from one of several acts of intimidation.)

With the Dissolution of the Monasteries in 1539 any tithes or rents previously paid to Bolton Priory were diverted to the King pending the sale of the estates over the next four years. There was a plea that the remaining chantry priests of Harewood Church should be able to receive some sort of pension as they were all over sixty years old and had no other income. For churchgoers from East Keswick and other parts of the parish, there was some continuity of religious life throughout the Reformation years. The incumbent, Father Percivall Ottelay, who had been appointed in 1517, remained in post until his death around 1566. After this the appointment of the Vicars of Harewood, which had been in the gift of the monastery since 1354, came under the patronage of Thomas Fairfax of Denton near Otley.

East Keswick Families

By the end of the Middle Ages feudal relationships in rural communities had broken down. In many places land changed hands frequently. Individuals had more opportunities to rent land and to play a greater role in the life of the village, although in East Keswick this was to be a gradual development. At the same time bureaucracy was increasing and there are more surviving records of ordinary people.

Lists of householders were drawn up either for taxation purposes, known as Lay Subsidy Rolls or, as in the case of the Muster Rolls of 1539, to assess the immediate availability of men and weapons in the event of invasion from France. The reliability of these records is variable but considered alongside other evidence we can begin to piece together a picture of village families. For example, the names in the Lay Subsidies are often the same as those listed as beneficiaries and witnesses of local wills which can give more information about status and relationships.

At the bottom of the social ladder were the labourers who worked for other people. Next came the small tenant farmer known as a husbandman. A yeoman was a more well to do tenant farmer, often with aspirations to be a gentleman. There is, of course, much that we do not know. For example, there is usually no clue as to where a particular family lived, but, until further research yields more information, we can allow our imagination to suggest comparisons between the life in the Tudor village and of the twenty-first century East Keswick.

In 1525 the Lay Subsidy Rolls listed fourteen taxpayers in East Keswick, compared with eleven in Bardsey and nineteen in Harewood. Bardsey yielded three times as much subsidy as East Keswick where, with the exception of two tenant farmers, all were taxed the minimum amount as labourers. Christopher Clough (the father of William involved in the Harewood Church riot) was one of these tenant farmers heading the list. He came from a Bardsey family and requested in his will that he be buried there with his parents. It was usual for people from East Keswick to be buried in their Parish Church in Harewood. When he died in 1529 Clough passed the lease he held from William Gascoigne to his son William along with eight oxen, other livestock, farming equipment, his bed and his bedclothes. Lesser bequests went to his wife and other three children and to his servant.

William Smythe, William Clough's partner in crime, is listed a labourer in the 1525 Subsidy but was described as yeoman in 1530. He was a witness to Christopher Clough's will and died himself in 1536 leaving a son, Richard, and a daughter.

There are seventeen names in the 1539 Muster Rolls. The six best equipped are described as archers having their own horses. Five inhabitants could provide some harness and a further six were listed as footmen with no harness.

Villagers may have thought that, because of the vast amount of money raised for the King by the Dissolution of the Monasteries, taxation would be kept to a minimum during the following decade. However Henry VIII's antagonistic attitude to the Scots involved continued expense, hence the use of various taxation strategies during the 1540s. Although these Lay Subsidy Rolls are thought to be less reliable as a tool for local history than earlier ones, there were now nearly twice as many names and nine new families in East Keswick. Again there were no wealthy resident landowners but a number of families appear to have progressed from labourers to tenant farmers.

The wills of some East Keswick families dated between 1530 and 1558 confirm a modest growth in prosperity. Some householders describe themselves as husbandmen, and a few aspired to the status of yeoman. One such was William Clough, who as a young man took part in the riot in Harewood Church. When he died he was able to pass on to his son William 'all my freholde lands with ... buildings ... being in Bardsayhill'. To his son John he left land he had leased from the estate of the late Lady Gascoigne. His younger children were to receive twenty pounds each when they came of age and the executors of his will were to receive horses and foals. Like his father he wanted to be buried in Bardsey Church, but mindful that East Keswick was in Harewood Parish he bequeathed two shillings to the vicar of Harewood to pray for his soul. In a will of 1560 Richard Appleyard was unusual at that time in that he gave an occupation other than farming. Describing himself as a clothier, his modest bequests included a black nag to his son and a cow to his daughter.

As few people could write, many wills appear to have been drafted by the same person, probably the vicar, or before the Dissolution, one of the chantry priests at Harewood. Bequests included crops, oxen, and harness but shorter wills comprised only a suitable religious introduction followed by provision to settle debts before dividing the residue among the children. The families were not large, mostly three or four children, and nearly all the Christian names would be familiar today, for example Richard, John, William, Thomas, Christopher, and Robert. Some girls' names were Elizabeth, Isabel, Dorothy, Margaret and Agnes.

A Lay Subsidy of 1588 provides less information for the local historian but it may be taken as indicating a small influx of more prosperous families. The tax assessment methods employed under Henry VIII were failing and this time only six families were required to pay the subsidy in East Keswick. Neither the Cloughs nor the Smythes, familiar from earlier records, are mentioned. Cuthbert Appleyard named in this Subsidy may have been related to Richard, the clothier who died the early 1560s (although he is not mentioned in the latter's will). The family name of John Sutton appears continuously in the records throughout the sixteenth and seventeenth centuries. In the 1620s they were labourers but thereafter may have become tenant farmers. The other four taxpayers in 1588, Thomas Wood, George Dawson, Henry Pullen and Henry Browne, may have recently moved from neighbouring villages.

From Tudors to Stuarts

It is thought that many rural populations took over one hundred years to recover from the economic decline and the plagues of the thirteenth century. Any attempt to estimate population numbers in East Keswick involves guesswork, but available evidence suggests there was little increase in population between the Poll Tax of 1379 when it was probably less than eighty, and the early sixteenth century. By 1550 this may have risen to over one hundred and the upward trend would have continued. Nationally, the period between 1550 and 1640 saw rapid population growth.

East Keswick remained a farming village and the land was still owned by non-resident landlords. However, local people increasingly had the opportunity to rent individual holdings. According to a document of 1569, what was left of the mediaeval estate or manor of East Keswick comprised twenty messuages (properties with land) and ten cottages. In 1601 another deed relating to the manor mentions the purchase of fifteen properties as well as pasture in the New Close and Cleeves Wood from a Henry Smith of Essex. Despite some enclosure the three large open fields, West Field, North Field and Beck Field, which had been the basis of mediaeval agriculture, still dominated the village.

Nearby in Harewood, the Gascoigne era came to an end in 1587. Gawthorpe had been established as a significant country estate although, following the death of the 'great earl' in 1551, his son brought things to a low ebb by riotous living in the five years before his own death. Margaret Gascoigne, the sole heir of the last William, had married Thomas Wentworth of Wentworth Woodhouse in South Yorkshire.

At Harewood Castle the Redmans and the Rythers had shared the inheritance since the end of the fourteenth century, but like other old landed families their status had declined after the Wars of the Roses. Around 1570 a James Ryther succeeded from a southern branch of that family. He married into a local family and proceeded to buy up Redman's share of the old Harewood estate clearly hoping to become a prestigious lord of the manor. However, his somewhat contemptuous attitude to his adopted county is unlikely to have endeared him to his neighbours. In 1588 he wrote a less than flattering account of Yorkshire, apparently to amuse his correspondent, Lord Burghley. He praised the industry and efficiency of the cloth merchants in the west of the county but had few good things to say about most other Yorkshiremen. He found the gentry coarse and uneducated compared with southerners. He commented that they were obsessed with hunting and in this he may have been criticising his former neighbour at Gawthorpe. A lack of education was also blamed for the love of gaming, alehouses and general idleness he found among the lower orders. He complained that the farmers were lazier than those in the south and he hints at overpopulation by the poor. He refers several times to the lack of sunshine in the north and this may have affected his temper and the tone of his writing.

He had, however, overstretched himself buying out the Redmans. William Wentworth, whose father had succeeded to Gawthorpe and who subsequently added Harewood to the family holding, explained that Ryther's 'proud overweening condition, albeitt he had especiall good giftes of nature, brought him to dye in the Flete for debt and his sonne Robert Rither to sell all his inheritance'.

William Wentworth's son Thomas became the first Earl of Strafford, the adviser to Charles I who later fell from favour and was executed in 1641. Earlier in his career he was appointed as President of the Council of the North, a sort of Star Chamber for the North of England.

We do not know how much East Keswick residents were aware of Strafford, their famous neighbour, or whether they shared his political sympathies. There was a mysterious incident 1629 when Thomas Wentworth was indirectly held responsible for a death in East Keswick. As a result he was required to surrender to the coroner the goods that were responsible for causing the death. We know that he was seeking to be excused from this obligation known as a *deodand*, and that he considered removing the offending goods from Harewood to prevent them being seized by the coroner, but there is no clue as to what the goods were or what had happened.

The most important administrative change brought about under the Tudors had been the development of the parish as the basic unit of civil government. Following the Reformation, the established parochial centres became responsible for registering births, marriages and deaths and distributing poor relief. A parish constable was appointed to report on law and order and the vestry was supposed to oversee the regulation of open fields. Records of baptisms for the Parish of Harewood survive from early in seventeenth century although there is gap between 1643 and 1660.

The village before the Civil War

Between 1614 and 1643 one hundred and forty children from East Keswick were baptised at Harewood Church. Some family names occur only once and there may have been considerable mobility between neighbouring villages. However a few apparently quite prosperous families of yeoman farmers, including the Dawsons, the Pullens and the Suttons, remained in the village for several generations. A new name in the records was Hopwood. At one time there were two George Hopwoods, one a tailor and one a saddletree maker and between them they had ten children. It is not clear whether they were related, but we do know that George the tailor belonged to a large family of farmers. Richard Hopwood, his brother, appears not to have married. He drew up a will in 1631, which, like other wills of the period, gives a brief glimpse of village life.

To his brother George and his children, Richard Hopwood left forty sheep, half of which were kept at Thorner and half at East Keswick. His widowed sister-in-law, Anne, was left an interest in the farm she occupied in East Keswick and annuities of twenty shillings and sixteen shillings to be paid out of the bequests he made to two of her children. (Anne's own will provided for each of her grandchildren to inherit 'a lamb of the best I have'). Richard's nephew Robert was to inherit the house, garden, close and land in the village that had recently been bought from a Richard Wilson of Linton while his niece Anne was left his portions of arable land in the three open fields, as well as a close in Cleeves Wood, which had recently been purchased from John Pullen.

Like Richard Hopwood, William Ingle had arable land in the three open fields and had also purchased several meadows in the Fitts. In his will drawn up in 1641 he describes himself as a saddletree maker although he would also have been a farmer. His land was divided among his four sons with the residue of his goods and chattels going to his wife Isabel.

Robert Pullen (or Pullaine) appears to have been a relatively young man when he made his will in 1640, 'being sick of body but of good and perfect remembrance'. He had six children, the youngest of whom was not yet baptised. His farmland was left to his two brothers on condition that they make provision for the maintenance of his wife Grace and the maintenance and tuition of his children. It is unlikely that there was any formal education available to village children at the time. Not until thirty years later is there a record of a schoolmaster living in East Keswick.

The baptism records provide little information about the occupations of the parents but there are a few comments that add some human detail. A daughter of George Dawson was 'baptised at home in time of necesssite', and John Ingle, son of William referred to above, was baptised at home 'at the time of great snow' in 1634. Other entries may have been the subject of gossip. Baby Innocent, the daughter of Elizabeth Gayton and Thomas Marshall, is described as a 'base child'. Samuel Walsh saw fit to record in the parish registers that baby William was 'affirmed by his wife in her labour to be the son one Mr Pannets a York draper'. We do not know what opportunities Mrs Walsh had to carry on this liaison, but it appears the family went on to have two legitimate children. Baby Grace Shires was born at East Keswick in 1638 and it is recorded that her father was a wanderer.

The Pullens and Dawsons were among yeomen involved in acquiring and enclosing small parcels of land and thus sharing in a growing prosperity based on changing farming patterns. During the first half of the sixteenth century a few aspired to the title of gentleman. Such persons would be unlikely to do any work with their hands and they would consider themselves socially above a yeoman. Brothers Edward and William Wythes were described as gentlemen, but their doubtful distinction was to be fined 2s 6d at the Quarter Sessions at Wakefield for assaulting Thomas Dawson.

East Keswick still had no church of its own so we can imagine regular worshippers trudging across the fields to Harewood once a week. By law all persons were required to attend church on Sundays but it is unlikely that this was strictly enforced. There is no indication of the religious persuasion of villagers apart from a Thomas Bankes whose son was baptised in 1636. In the register he is described as a 'clerke of East Keswick and lecturer at Harewood'. Lecturers at the time were Puritan preachers who travelled around the country preaching against the high church tendencies of the Anglican bishops.

The Parish was responsible for looking after its own poor and for this it relied upon charitable giving and benefactions. In 1608 Richard Dawson of Collingham, who was probably related to the Dawsons of East Keswick, left the income from 'certain lands and tenements lying in Clifford and East Keswick to the poor of the township of East Keswick'. We have no evidence of who in East Keswick received charity but we do know it was not always given unconditionally. In 1631 the clerk of Harewood stipulated that no children born out of wedlock were to benefit from his bequest to the villages in the Parish. It was to be used to place a boy or girl as apprentice, but East Keswick's turn came only once every ten years or so. Elizabeth Harrison, a widow from East Keswick, made provision in her will for the poor of the Parish of Harewood. Five pounds was to be given directly to the Church and another five to be handed out to the poor by her daughter during the year after her death.

The Civil War

West Yorkshire was the centre of opposition to the King in the North of England at the beginning of the Civil War. Lord Fairfax of Denton near Otley and his son Sir Thomas Fairfax, the Parliamentarian, were able to recruit large numbers of men from the clothing towns of Bradford, Leeds and Halifax. Few recruits came from rural areas but villagers from places like East Keswick could not have been unaware of the movement of soldiers around the area between 1642 and 1644. One night in the autumn of 1642 a loud explosion may well have been heard in East Keswick, possibly causing some panic among the inhabitants. It also terrified the royalist troops who had ventured from their stronghold at York to attack Fairfax's depot at Wetherby. The King's men had in fact blown up a powder magazine and mistaken the explosion for cannon fire, causing them to beat a retreat to York.

Fairfax later held out against Royalists at Leeds and captured Wakefield in May 1643. Reporting this victory to the House of Commons, Fairfax described how the continued presence of the Royalists in West Yorkshire was causing a severe shortage of food, almost total disruption of trade and increasing poverty. In June Fairfax was defeated at Aldwalton Moor near Bradford and the Parliamentarians retreated to Hull. The size of the armies continued to increase and when, a year later, over forty thousand soldiers assembled for the Battle of Marston Moor for the biggest battle of the Civil War, there must have been a significant impact for miles around. Six days before battle commenced on 2nd July Prince Rupert assembled his army in Skipton in preparation for the relief of the besieged city of York. The route he eventually took may have passed near East Keswick as he proceeded to Knaresborough before approaching York from the north. York surrendered to Parliament on 16th July 1644 after which the conflict moved away from the county.

The village 1645 - 1700

Between 1649 and 1660 religious and political leaders attempted to enforce a strict moral code and to change social habits and customs. Minor offences such as drunkenness, swearing and gambling were legislated against and church festivals were regarded as sinful. People were told they should be fasting rather than celebrating and they were required by law to attend church on Sunday. Many in rural communities tried to ignore these measures and greeted with great relief the more relaxed approach after the Restoration of Charles II in 1660. In East Keswick, however, some at least were influenced by Quaker teachings. Others remained faithful to the established church and played an active part in the life of the Parish Church at Harewood.

Alongside religion was a traditional belief in witchcraft, which went back hundreds of years. If a misfortune such as the an unexplained loss of corn or cattle occurred in the countryside there was a tendency to lay the blame on any man, or more often a woman, who had previously cursed the unlucky individual. Government records tell us of an Elizabeth Melton of Collingham, who had been convicted of witchcraft and had received a pardon in 1597. As well as those actually convicted, there were people known as 'cunning folk' who claimed to have occult powers. By the end of the seventeenth century, so-called scientific tests for witchcraft were taken less seriously although there was still widespread superstition in the countryside. Various supernatural creatures were thought to be active after dark. Will-o'-the-Wisp was supposed to live near Keswick Beck, leaving the marsh at night to lift the latches on doors. Goblins also came out at night, frequenting the area above the River Wharfe where once the gallows stood. Another story tells of the Wike Hill ghost early in the eighteenth century. Frank Sturr lived in a thatched house at the bottom of Main Street. He was a dubious character regularly involved in petty crime. He frequently rode to Bradford in the hours of darkness on his fast horse, travelling via Wike Moor. At a certain point, the branches of a rowan tree hung over the track. One night as Frank approached the branch came down. According to the story, Sturr shook his fist in anger crying out 'then thoo's theer agean, oade witch'.

In 1643 local administration had been thrown into disarray by the Civil War and parish records for Harewood have not survived. With the restoration of Charles II, baptism and marriage registers were resumed, providing us with more information about the inhabitants of East Keswick. There is also the potential for more detailed research into the changing rural scene.

The baptism records comprise only brief entries but occasionally they suggest some village gossip. In 1674 the schoolmaster, Robert Turner, surely aroused comment when he was named as the father of an illegitimate son born to Ester Ingle *alias* 'Totty.' There may also have been an interesting story behind the birth of baby Elizabeth, the daughter of 'a strange woman' born at George Roodes' house.

Around thirty new families appear to have moved to East Keswick between 1660 and 1700. Many were probably of modest means, but Thomas Steele, who had three children, lived in a fairly substantial property which may have been have part of a mini building boom. Houses were becoming more comfortable and stone replaced many timber buildings. A hearth tax was introduced which taxed all but the very poor households according to the number of fireplaces. In 1672 there were thirty-six households in East Keswick, twenty-three of which were more modest dwellings with only one hearth. The most substantial property belonged to John Pullen (or Pullaine)

East Keswick Hearth Tax 1672

Christopher Hopwwod..........2	Robert Sutton, or heirs..........2	Richard Allerton..........1
John Pullen..........5	William Pullen, jun...........3	James Gayton..........1
Matthew Stevenson..........2	John Labourne..........2	James Harrison..........1
Ann Dawson..........1	Thomas Cowper..........1	William Clithery..........1
George Hopwood..........1	Thomas Mawde..........2	Thomas Stele..........1
William Inman..........2	Matthew Jackson..........1	William Hodgson..........2
William Teale..........1	Thomas Steele..........4	John Pullan..........1
Richard Dawson..........1	William Ingle..........1	William Hodgson, sen...........1
Thomas Hancocke..........1	William Rothery..........1	Matthew Teale..........1
Henry Hodgson..........3	Robert Sutton, jun...........1	William Thornhill..........1
Widow Laveron..........2	Ann Thornhill..........2	Robert Ingle..........1
Joseph Turner..........1	Brian Morris..........1	Christopher Brigland..........1

who had five. Was this the old moated manor house, or had this already fallen into disuse? William Pullen, who was probably John's cousin, had a house with three hearths and was named as the village constable. This was a parish appointment involving a number of duties including supervising the collection of taxes, apprehending suspected criminals, and removing itinerant beggars.

At the end of the seventeenth century East Keswick was still a small village though with a growing number of moderately prosperous farmers. Based on the Hearth Tax returns in 1672 an estimate of population would be in the region of one hundred and fifty to one hundred and seventy. Later George Ogden, Vicar of Harewood, stated that 'upon diligent enquiry made in 1676' he had counted ninety-five communicants from East Keswick.

A note on sources

As with the previous chapter much of the material for the Tudor and Stuart period is derived from records published by the Yorkshire Archaeological Society and Thoresby Society. Other books cited there also cover this period. Additional material was found in two books in the Camden Miscellany series, the *Wentworth Papers* and the *Plompton Papers*. Harewood baptism records are published by the Parish Record Society and the seventeenth century wills were studied from the originals in the Borthwick Institute in York. The Civil war is covered in *The Original Memoirs of Sir Thomas Fairfax* and in *The Readiness of the People* by AJ Hopper.

3

Land ownership 1739-1951: the Lascelles factor

Land has traditionally represented economic, social and political status and power in British society. Through the ages rich families have sought to gain status, both locally and nationally, through the acquisition of property and entry into the landed gentry and aristocracy. For about two hundred years from the late 1600s the general trend was for the landed estates to accumulate and consolidate their holdings at the expense of smaller landowners. In the late nineteenth century the traditional link between land ownership and political power began to weaken. The early years of the twentieth century witnessed the beginning of a substantial change in the pattern of land ownership, with the break-up of many large estates. Post First World War tax changes accelerated this 'revolution' in land owning.

East Keswick, in common with Dunkeswick, Weeton, Weardley, Wike, Wigton, Harewood and Alwoodley, was a 'township' within the Parish of Harewood extending to 1,225 acres of land. In many respects the village mirrored national trends in land ownership. The Lascelles family of Harewood began their purchase of land in East Keswick in 1739, gradually increasing the acreage over the next two centuries, until the final dispersal of their holdings in the mid twentieth century. This chapter aims to trace the changing pattern of the ownership of land in East Keswick with particular emphasis on the rise and fall of the Lascelles connection that occurred during the period 1739 to 1951.

With wealth derived mainly from merchant trading in the West Indies Henry Lascelles purchased the estates of Gawthorpe and Harewood, valued at more than £63,000, from the trustees and executors of John Boulter. Included in these estates was farmland in

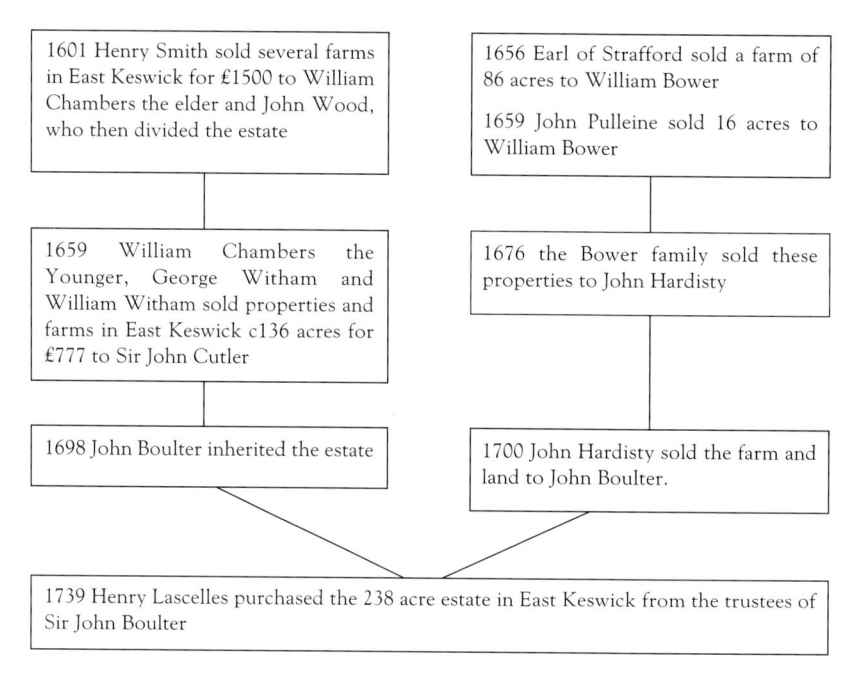

East Keswick

1601 - 1739 Ownership of Land in East Keswick Purchased by Henry Lascelles

| 1601 Henry Smith sold several farms in East Keswick for £1500 to William Chambers the elder and John Wood, who then divided the estate | 1656 Earl of Strafford sold a farm of 86 acres to William Bower |
| | 1659 John Pulleine sold 16 acres to William Bower |

| 1659 William Chambers the Younger, George Witham and William Witham sold properties and farms in East Keswick c136 acres for £777 to Sir John Cutler | 1676 the Bower family sold these properties to John Hardisty |

| 1698 John Boulter inherited the estate | 1700 John Hardisty sold the farm and land to John Boulter. |

| 1739 Henry Lascelles purchased the 238 acre estate in East Keswick from the trustees of Sir John Boulter |

East Keswick totalling 238 acres. The purchase also included unspecified manorial rights as Lord of the Manor over East Keswick Common (305 acres), the common pasture of Ox Close (42 acres) and the Free Rents, paid by freeholders, amounting to seven shillings a year. The diagram opposite outlines the various owners of the 238 acres in the previous century.

Between 1739 and 1796 the acreage of farmland owned by the Lascelles family in East Keswick increased to 627.

With the exception of seven acres sold by Joseph Midgley, a yeoman living in East Keswick, all the Lascelles acquisitions in the eighteenth century were from absentee landlords, the majority of whom were described as gentlemen. Several of the vendors appear to have sold the property upon inheritance, while for others the ownership of land may have been principally for investment reasons. The Lascelles were not alone in buying land in East Keswick for rental income rather than to farm directly. However over the first eighty years their greater purchasing power enabled them to outbid most other potential buyers.

Lascelles' first purchase was in 1745. An estimated 25 acres were bought from Thomas

Midgley, gentleman, of Harewood, son and heir of Samuel Midgley, gentleman, of Alwoodley. This was the only land purchase by the Lascelles during their first decade at Harewood, despite several farms coming onto the market.

In the 1750s and early 1760s the Lascelles family increased their land purchases in East Keswick, possibly taking advantage of the widespread depression in agriculture. However, although dominating the property market at this time, the Harewood Estate did not buy up all the available land. Several smaller properties were bought by yeomen of East Keswick and in 1752 the sizeable tenanted property belonging to the Dinsdale family of Otley was bought by another absentee landlord, seeking investment in land ownership.

In 1750 the Lascelles family bought a property of about 25 acres from Henry Whitaker, a gentleman of Otley. Only fifteen years earlier Whitaker, then living at Gawthorpe, had bought the farm from William Cowper, a tallow chandler of Weardley.

In the middle of the century Lascelles acquired Steel's land which, though only a few acres, was important for its location next to Ox Close and other Harewood property. The Steel family had been selling quite a lot of property in East Keswick around this time as Benjamin Steel, heir to the property, was already farming elsewhere.

In 1752 Joshua Wilson, gentleman, of Pontefract, sold a farm of approximately 50 acres to Lascelles. This land had previously belonged to a succession of non-resident landlords.

Lascelles bought 'Bonnel's Old Farm' in 1755, though the deed only mentions closes and land totalling 12¾ acres. William Bonnell was a gentleman living in Lancaster, and heir of Thomas Bonnell, gentleman of York, deceased. Thomas Bonnell had only owned the land for a few years, having bought it from Steel in 1751. The exchange of deeds took place at The Angel Hotel in Halifax between Bonnell and Harewood's agent, Popplewell.

An interesting story surrounds the sale of a 25-acre farm and malt kiln to Lascelles by the three daughters of James Tupman. Tupman had lived in Methley, near Castleford, at least as far back as 1738/9 and at the time of his death in 1759 his son-in-law, Thomas Atkinson, a cooper, farmed the holding in East Keswick. In 1760, Bradley and Ellis, collectors of the land tax in East Keswick, complained that Atkinson 'absolutely refuses' to pay the £1-5s land tax. A warrant, signed by the JPs, authorised them to levy the sum 'by Distress and Sale of the Goods and Chattells of the said Thomas Atkinson', who was by this time living on a farm in Oulton near Rothwell.

'We do hereby authorise you to break open in the day time, any house where

Land Ownership in East Keswick in 1796

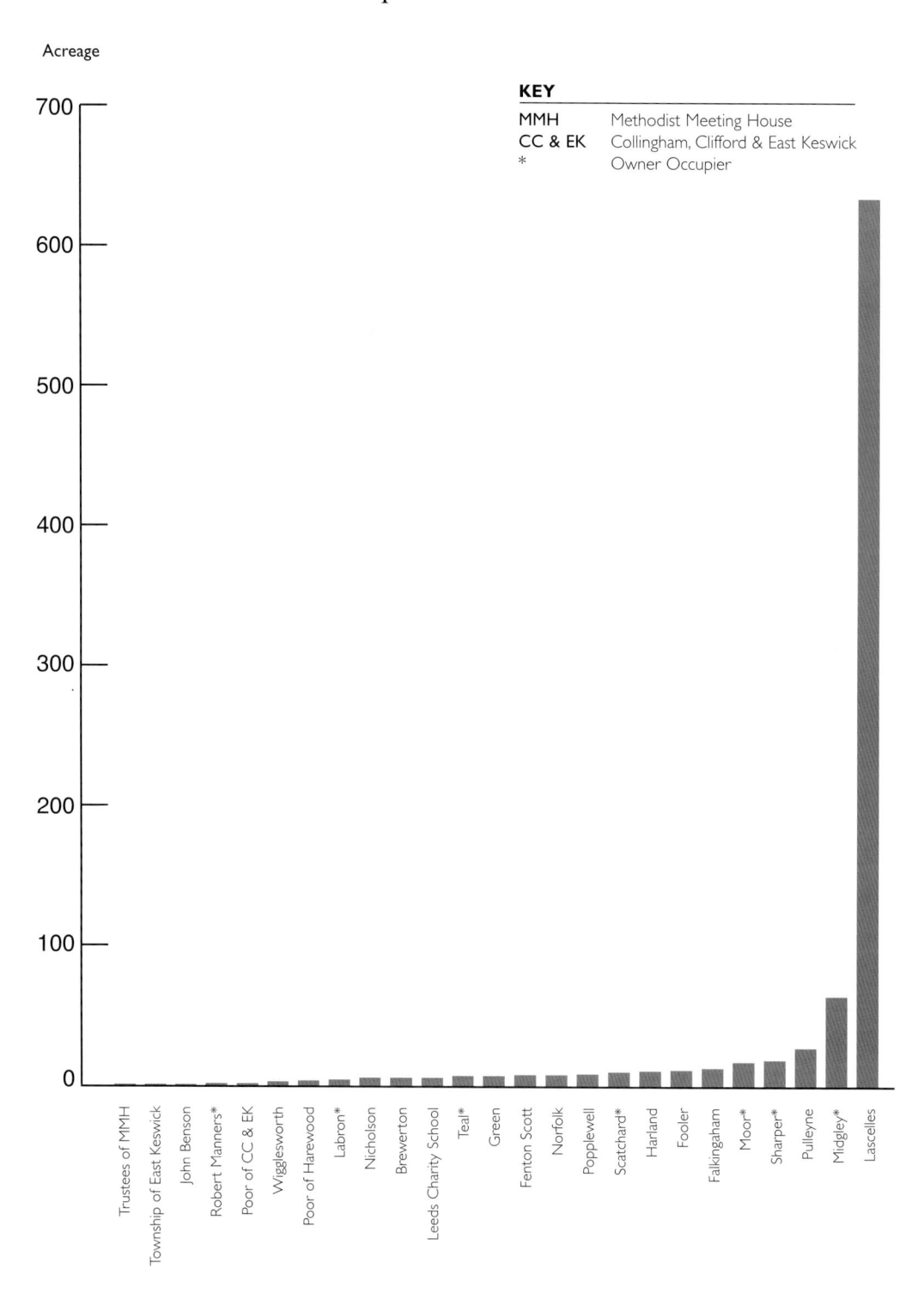

KEY

MMH	Methodist Meeting House
CC & EK	Collingham, Clifford & East Keswick
*	Owner Occupier

Acreage values shown from 0 to 700.

Owners (left to right): Trustees of MMH, Township of East Keswick, John Benson, Robert Manners*, Poor of CC & EK, Wigglesworth, Poor of Harewood, Labron*, Nicholson, Brewerton, Leeds Charity School, Teal*, Green, Fenton Scott, Norfolk, Popplewell, Scatchard*, Harland, Fooler, Falkingaham, Moor*, Sharper*, Pulleyne, Midgley*, Lascelles.

any such goods are, calling to your assistance the Constable of the said Township of Oulton.'

Another farm of 40 acres was added to the Harewood estate in East Keswick in 1763, with the purchase of a farm and malt kiln from John Ritchie, gentleman, of Otley. It was noted, possibly by the Harewood agent, that:

'This farm is well let, the barn and malt kiln in bad repair, No improvement to be made but from the lands (as well the Inclosures as field land) lying intermixt with Mr. Lascelles, for of itself the farm lyes strangely dispursed yet if Mr. Ritchieu will take £750 for it ….upon the whole [it] can not be a bad purchase considering the chance of enclosing the Common.'

Ritchie had bought the estate eleven years earlier in 1752 from the Dinsdale family of Otley. William Dinsdale, a maltster, had been living in Otley in 1738/9, so for at least 23 years this farm had been rented out by absentee landowners. Thomas Maude, acting for Ritchie, used the occasion to curry favour with Lascelles.

'I may also remark as private history, that the notion for disposing of it in your favour, first came from me….nor is his plea for selling it, founded on any want of money, as I know he is a proprietor in the funds. I should think myself much wanting in the obligations I owe for your many distinguishing marks of favour, did I not on all occasions endeavour to approve myself.'

There was a lull in the purchasing activities of the Lascelles in East Keswick in the following twenty years, a period when the Lascelles were devoting their financial resources to the building and resplendent furnishing of Harewood House and gardens. In a letter concerning the proposed purchase of land in the North Riding in 1761, Edwin Lascelles, son and heir of Henry, had described country people as 'idiots' for paying exorbitant prices for small pieces of land. For whatever reason Lascelles did not buy two substantial properties in East Keswick for sale in the early 1770s. In 1771 Bacon Morritt of York, owner of extensive properties in West Yorkshire, including the Manor of Egbrough, sold his property in East Keswick to Joseph Midgley the younger, who was already farming his own land in the village. The following year John Gott of Woodhall in the parish of Calverley purchased property in the village from William Meyer of Baildon and his wife.

Land acquisition by the Lascelles recommenced in East Keswick in 1786, with the purchase of two sizeable estates, both from non-resident landowners. Lascelles paid John Gott £1,050 for a 33-acre farm and bought a 50-acre farm from George Ward of

Land Purchases by the Lascelles Family in the 18th Century

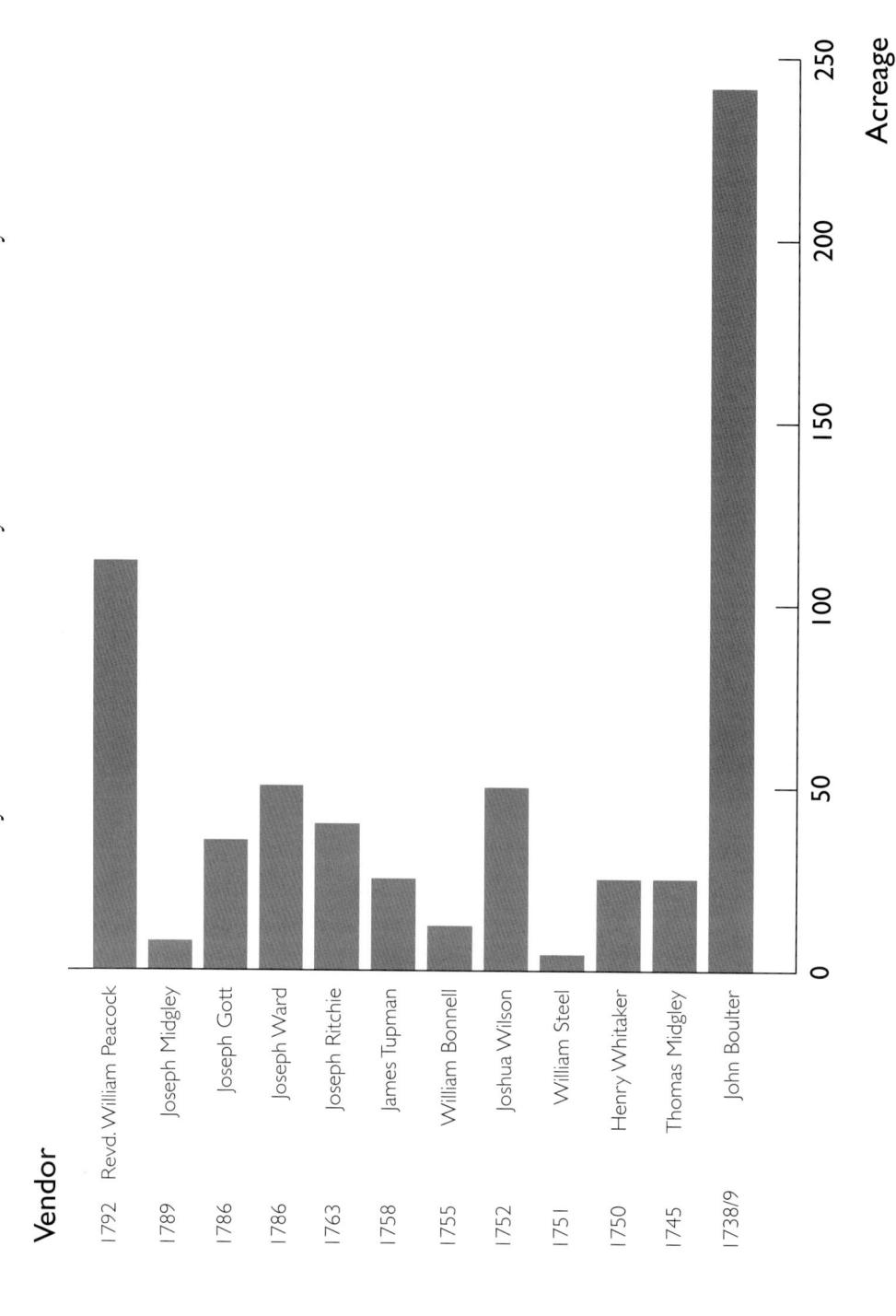

Vendor	Year	Acreage (approx.)
Revd. William Peacock	1792	115
Joseph Midgley	1789	10
Joseph Gott	1786	40
Joseph Ward	1786	50
Joseph Ritchie	1763	45
James Tupman	1758	25
William Bonnell	1755	15
Joshua Wilson	1752	50
William Steel	1751	5
Henry Whitaker	1750	25
Thomas Midgley	1745	25
John Boulter	1738/9	240

Northallerton, whose family had owned the property for many years.

In 1792 Edwin Lascelles became owner of the second largest property in East Keswick. This estate of 122 acres with three farms and five cottages had belonged to the Breary - Mitford family for most of the eighteenth century. William Breary, rector of Guiseley, had bought the estate from William Ingle at some date before 1712. In 1745 the property was inherited by a female descendant, wife of Daniel Mitford, an apothecary and surgeon in Northallerton. On the death of Daniel Mitford, Elizabeth, his only child and heir, inherited the property and it was her husband, the Revd. William Peacock of Northallerton, who sold the property to Lascelles.

By 1796 over two thirds of the farmland in East Keswick was in the possession of the Harewood Estate, with the remaining 239 acres divided amongst 24 other landowners, many of whom held less than ten acres.

At the end of the century, when East Keswick Common was enclosed and went into private ownership, the size of the Harewood estate in East Keswick increased from 627 to 764 acres.

Purchases in the following two decades further consolidated the Harewood holdings. In 1803 a smallholding was bought from members of the Green family, living in Huddersfield and Liverpool. Lascelles bought small plots of land from William Teal of East Keswick in 1809 and from the heirs of Mr Popplewell in 1812. There is a reference to John Benson of East Keswick selling property to Lascelles in 1809. A larger purchase of a 30-acre farm was made in 1811. The sellers were Joseph and William Wigglesworth, farmers, and John Pullein, gentleman, all absentee landlords. The property had been in the Pullein family since before 1709 and the family had been absentee landlords for many years. The last land purchase in this period was in 1815, from the heirs of John Falkingham, yeoman and 'late of Cattal'. This land had been in the hands of an absentee landlord since Falkingham bought it in 1769.

The next fifty years were relatively quiet, with few land transactions by the Harewood Estate. In 1849 £330 was paid to Mr Teal and in 1854 £55 to Miss Ann Bullock for lands in East Keswick.

A more active land purchasing strategy was adopted in the late 1870s when Moorsom, agent to Lord Harewood, seemed intent on buying out owners of land lying adjacent to Harewood property. He negotiated purchases of land from Groves and Webster in 1877 and from the Taylor family in 1883. With the purchases of small pieces of land between Harewood Road and The Fitts from David Parker, William Midgley, Mr Moon's Trustees and The Leeds Charity, he consolidated the Harewood holdings in this part of East

Land Ownership in East Keswick 1886

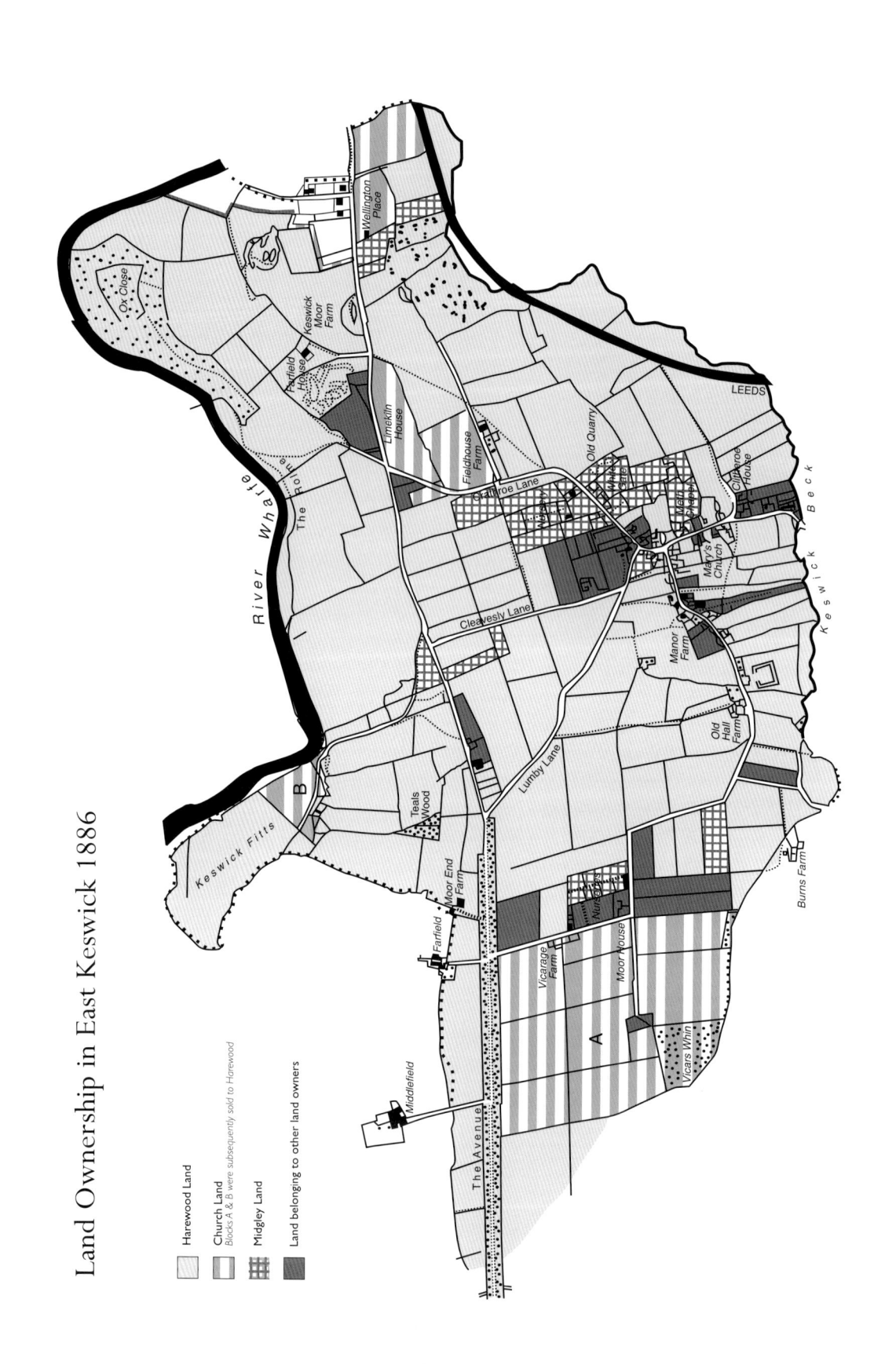

- Harewood Land
- Church Land
  Blocks A & B were subsequently sold to Harewood
- Midgley Land
- Land belonging to other land owners

Keswick. Moorsom's correspondence in the matter of Parker's sale illustrates the zeal and psychology the agent applied to his work:

> 'I have had David Parker here this morning about his small field in East Keswick…He wants to sell and I want to buy. I have bid him £200 and he says he can't take that…He says Mr Turner (solicitor) is the mortgagee and wants his money on the 1st January next! so I think we have him safe!…The other little bits adjoining I want to get also - Moons I hear may be had.'

The solicitors in Leeds replied that Parker had asked for £300 - they offered £225 - he said he'd accept £240 and no less. 'We cannot apparently get lower and we await your instructions!!!'

The following day Moorsom replied ' I met David Parker on the road this morning…I said - What - he bid you £225 and you didn't take it? No - he said there was a man in Leeds would give him more - very well - I said - go and get it from him - no - he said - I mean you to have it - then I said you will certainly get no more than…£225 - and there we parted. I have no fear that anyone else will give him more - it is as good as ours -'

Two weeks later the Leeds office wrote that Parker had been in and accepted the offer.

In 1882 Harewood bought five acres of land in East Keswick from the Leeds School Charity for 600 guineas. Writing to the London office, Moorsom had obviously urged the strategic importance of buying the land but unlike the Parker purchase was unable to strike such a favourable bargain. Nicholls wrote from London that Lord Harewood agreed to the purchase.

> 'I have no doubt it was very important to have these lands and that the owners - specifically being a charity - declined to sell unless their costs were paid, but of course one never likes to have to pay the other side's costs.'

The map on the previous page visually emphasises the extent to which Harewood was dominating land ownership in East Keswick by the 1880s.

In the 1890s land owned by the Church came onto the market (the church had been allotted 165 acres at the time of enclosure in lieu of certain tithes). Harewood Estate bought only eight acres of Church land in 1894 for £520. Clearly at this time the Estate was unwilling or unable to increase its land holding in East Keswick for, in the same year, 148 acres of Church land were sold to other purchasers. Vicarage Farm off Moor Lane - 113 acres of 'formerly ancient glebe land' - was sold at auction to Charles Foster Ryder Esq. of Leeds for £3,220 in 1894.

Sale of Farms in East Keswick by the Harewood Estate 1950/1

1950 Field Head Farm (175 acres) sold to Mr E Lupton, tenant, £8250

1950 Manor House Farm (170 acres) sold to J J Dalby, tenant, £7900

1950 Old Hall Farm (41 acres) sold to J J Dalby, tenant, £4200

1951 Avenue Nurseries (41 acres) sold to J W Firth, tenant,

1951 Keswick Moor Farm (207 acres), sold to Kirkham Investment Trust Ltd, City Chambers, Leeds. Tenant: Herbert Hall

1951 Vicarage Farm (113 acres) withdrawn from sale at £3000. Sold in 1960 to D A Wild of Nunfield Fritchley in Derbyshire for £4400. Tenant: G S Briggs

1951 Accommodation Land (87 acres) sold to M Harrison and Co, Post Hill Quarries, Farnley. Tenant: J J Dalby. The purchaser also bought Farfield Farm (117 acres) in Harewood. Tenant: Walter Pratt.

1951 Moor End Farm (32 acres) sold to R V Smith, butcher, Leeds for £3850. Tenant: M Rhodes

Harewood farms with a small amount of land in East Keswick

1951 Stockton Farm (143 acres) sold to J Dunhill, builder, East Keswick, and J S Tomlinson, local government officer, Leeds. Tenant: J Harland

1951 Middlefield Farm (160 acres) sold to Alfred Watson, Cowthorpe Hall Farm, Wetherby for £7100. Tenant: A M and W R Rhodes.

By the turn of the century Harewood Estate was again in a position to make major purchases, such as Farfield, a 90-acre estate bordering on East Keswick, bought from the Mother and Sisters of the Beamsley Hospital for £5,470. The purchase of Vicarage Farm for £4,130 by the Harewood Estate in 1902 marked the last major acquisition of land in East Keswick by the Lascelles family.

In the twentieth century, Harewood Estate showed no further inclination to increase its land ownership in East Keswick, even when land, such as that belonging to the Midgley family, came onto the market. The Midgleys, who had been the second largest property owners in East Keswick after the Lascelles in the nineteenth century, had disappeared from the scene by the 1930s. Their property was sold off gradually and in a piecemeal fashion as members of the Midgley family died, leaving property to executors who lived at a distance from East Keswick.

In 1919 Harewood put 10,000 acres of their Estate in North Yorkshire onto the market, an example of the widespread sale of landed estates, which led commentators at the time to declare 'England is changing hands'. However sales of Harewood property in East Keswick were few and of insignificant size - an old cottage and garden in 1903, an acre of land to Wetherby Rural District Council in 1910, a further acre in 1922 and a dwelling house and school in 1913. In 1933 the Council bought 1½ acres for housing for £250 and a further plot of land in 1945 for £20. A & S Tindall paid £110 for the Café in East Keswick in 1933, and a Mr West bought a plot of land in the village in 1943, with a further purchase four years later. In 1944 the churchyard was extended with land purchased from the Harewood Estate.

After 1945 tax changes increased the pressures on landowners to sell their estates. This time the impact on East Keswick in terms of land ownership was dramatic. Following Lord Harewood's death in 1947, death duties of nearly 70% had to be paid so in 1950 and 1951 approximately 962 acres of Harewood property in the village were sold as part of a 14,600 acre sale of Harewood Estate land in Yorkshire. The land was sold in 25 Lots, the great majority being sold to sitting tenants. However it is evident that non-farming people or concerns bought a substantial acreage, particularly of land and farms outside the main village.

The value of property in East Keswick spiralled over the last fifty years of the millennium. A 113-acre farm in East Keswick (Vicarage Farm) sold for £4,400 in 1951. Twenty years later P Asquith of Reighton House, Moor Lane, paid £28,300 for a 94-acre farm (Burns Farm), while in 1997/8 the asking price for Field House, a 218-acre arable and stock farm in Crabtree Lane, was in excess of £920,000.

Ironically, the nearer we get to the present day, the more difficult it becomes to determine who owns the land. There has been no national survey of landownership since 1915, following Lloyd George's 1909 - 1910 Finance Act, which proposed a tax on land values.

A note on sources

Information about land ownership came from two main sources - the Harewood Archives, in particular the Deeds material, deposited by the Earl of Harewood in the West Riding Archives at Sheepscar, Leeds, and the summaries of Deeds, 1704-1970, at the West Riding Registry of Deeds at Wakefield. Harewood Estate kindly allowed access to its twentieth century copy conveyances of property in East Keswick. Leeds Reference Library has the 1950/51 Sales details of the Harewood Estate in Eask Keswick. Other than a map of Harewood Estate c.1698, showing only the western edge of the Township of East Keswick, the earliest surviving detailed map of the village dates from the early nineteenth century. The Enclosure Map and Award 1801-1803 are available for public viewing at West Yorkshire Archives at both Sheepscar and Wakefield. The earliest Ordnance Survey Map showing the village in detail is mid-nineteenth century. As the church received compensation for the loss of tithes at the time of enclosure there was no Tithe Award of map for East Keswick following the Tithe Act of 1836.

4

Farming in the Eighteenth Century

East Keswick has remained a rural village and, until relatively recently, most of its inhabitants worked in farming and associated agricultural activities. This was against a background of a twenty-fold increase in population nationally and the huge expansion of towns and manufacturing, transforming the country from a predominantly rural agricultural economy to an urban industrial one.

Farming did not remain immune to these changes. Although developments in agriculture were more gradual, village life in East Keswick has altered beyond recognition over the last three hundred years. The following chapters will trace these changes, looking first at the organisation of agriculture in the eighteenth century, based on the centuries-old open field system. Chapter 5 outlines events which led to the disappearance of the old farming scene and heralded the arrival of a landscape that in many respects we recognise today. The chapter also examines the nature of farming in what had effectively become an Estate village, with most of the farmers tenants of the Harewood Estate. Chapter 6 details the farms and nurseries in East Keswick from the late nineteenth century.

In 1796 a survey of East Keswick identified 44 properties, 27 of which were farms and smallholdings. There were also several shops, a smithy, a brewhouse, a malt kiln, two public houses, a Methodist meeting house and a Quaker burial ground. It was a mixed farming area, with crops grown for human and animal consumption. All but three of the seventeen farms belonging to Harewood had mistals (cow houses) while pig cotes/sties are mentioned on seven of the farms. There were fifty-seven farm horses in the village.

Agricultural Landscape in East Keswick 1796 *(Based on 1801 enclosure map)*

- Township Boundary
- East Keswick Common 303 acres
- Ox Close/New Close 48 acres
- West Field
- Beck Field   299 acres
- North Field
- The Fitts
- Bell Crook
- Areas of enclosed fields 567 acres
- Old enclosed fields

The community farmed several distinct agricultural areas in the village in the eighteenth century.

Farming in the Open Fields

A significant proportion of the arable land in the village was farmed under the 'open-field system'. Land was farmed and crops grown on individually owned strips in three large fields - Beck Field, North Field and West Field, known as the Open or Township Fields.

Using a single furrow non-reversible plough, the farmer ploughed a strip of ground, which was known as a 'land' in East Keswick. Here land was approximately a quarter of an acre, though obviously the lands varied in size according to the nature of the terrain and soil type.

A number of these 'lands' grouped together was called a flatt or furshott. The three large open fields in East Keswick were made up of a number of these smaller fields. For example, Beck Field comprised twelve smaller fields, individually described with names such as Haggerham Head, Broad Gate, Crooked Rows, Joanney Crabtree, and ranging in size from one to eight acres. Without a pre-enclosure map, however, it is impossible to visualise either the layout of these smaller fields within the Township fields or that of the lands within the small fields.

Traditionally the length of the furrow was 220 yards (a furlong) though this would vary according to local conditions. The individual furrow and the strip of land would gradually assume a sinuous reverse S-shape as the oxen or horse imperceptibly altered course as it approached the headland to turn round. Interestingly several of the boundaries of the ancient enclosures in West Field even today show this shape; the hedging on the west side of Crabtree Lane, running parallel with Allerton Drive, is a particularly good example of a hedge which is over two hundred years old. We can infer the length and direction of the strips in the open field from these old boundary hedges; it makes sense that the orientation of the strips in West Field - in a roughly north-south direction - was so designed as to get maximum sunlight on the soil and crops.

There were no hedges within the Open Fields, though hedging sometimes marked the boundary between two Open Fields. There still survives a stretch of banked hedge formerly marking the boundary between North and Beck Fields, which goes eastwards from the apex of the triangular piece of commemoration land on Crabtree Lane. The old hedge dividing East Keswick Common from West Field can be identified on the 1851

The surviving boundary hedge between North and Beck Fields

map but has disappeared now. A change in the banking and hedge along Moor Lane marks the southern end of this old boundary. It is interesting to observe, both on maps and 'on the ground', the difference between those roads, lanes and hedges that pre-date the enclosures and are therefore more than two hundred years old, and those made and planted at the time of enclosure. The latter are straight and of uniform width whereas the older roads and hedges are narrower and more winding.

The farmers in East Keswick cultivated strips of land scattered in each of the Township Fields. In 1711, for example, Samuel Midgley's farm had 3¼ acres in five separate blocks in the three Township Fields. In 1726 William Teal bought four acres which was split into seven blocks of land, also situated in the three open fields, only one of which exceeded one acre in size. By the eighteenth century farmers were often farming more than one 'land' in a block but even then the area very rarely exceeded one acre. For example, only one of the seventeen blocks of land in the Township Fields, farmed by Thomas Atkinson in the 1750s, measured more than one acre.

In the days before artificial fertilisers arable land was left fallow or uncultivated in order for the soil to recuperate. In 1796 the surveyor of East Keswick claimed that 'no other mode of culture is thought of by the tenant but the old obsolete one of 2 crops and a fallow which has been so long the practice that the soil is completely worn out.'

There was regional variation in the extent to which root crops and sown grasses were introduced into the cropping system of the open fields. According to the 1749-56 Accounts, James and Thomas Bradley of East Keswick were supplying Harewood Estate with clover, vetches and beans, in addition to wheat, oats and straw. The surveys of East Keswick in 1796 and 1797 do not detail the land use on the open fields, other than as arable. It is therefore impossible to assess the crop rotation used in the open fields.

The open field system would require a degree of communal farming, which was regulated by the manorial courts. Many of the manorial regulations were concerned with boundary issues. In 1738 William Steele junior was ordered to 'plash his hedg, scower his dich against his Clays in the north field betwixt (13th October) and the 2 of Febry next...' and in 1740 James Harrison was under pain to 'make a sufficient fence betwixt his garth and James Bradley Claythera Garth.' In 1742 Issac Bayle was presented 'for removing a mear stone lying betwixt Mr Thomas Midgley and William Steele' and fined 5/6d. Trespassing and the regulation of rights of way were other concerns of the courts. In 1739 it was ruled that 'no manner of person do make a way over James Bradlay Hollywell Close butt where the ancant way lyeth.' Stray animals were secured in the village pinfold; in 1745 Robert Pettie was fined two shillings for 'breaking the Pinfould lock and taking out his Goods by force.'

In addition to the cultivation of crops, grazing in the open fields played an important part in the farming economy of eighteenth century East Keswick. It provided manure for the land as well as extra food for the animals. The fallows and the stubble after harvest provided grazing. The ownership of this valuable asset was protected by manorial customs and regulations. People with no formal rights to graze the fields were fined for infringing this rule. In 1743 it was ruled that 'no person do tent or tether in the Town field but where they have a right' and in 1750 none shall 'tent or tether any cattle between White Yate and Burton Yate or any place in the fields but where they have a right...' The manorial rules were also designed to limit the use of grazing and prevent overstocking of the land. A pain of 1738 'layd that ...no person put into any fallow field any more than three sheep for one gate or three sheep for one acre.'

Farming in the Common Pastures

The Fitts, New Close and Bell Crook were known as stinted or common pastures. Stinted pastures were areas of permanent meadow land where there was shared grazing at specific times of the year in accordance with manorial custom. The term 'common' did not imply common ownership; indeed Bell Crook and the Fitts were divided into

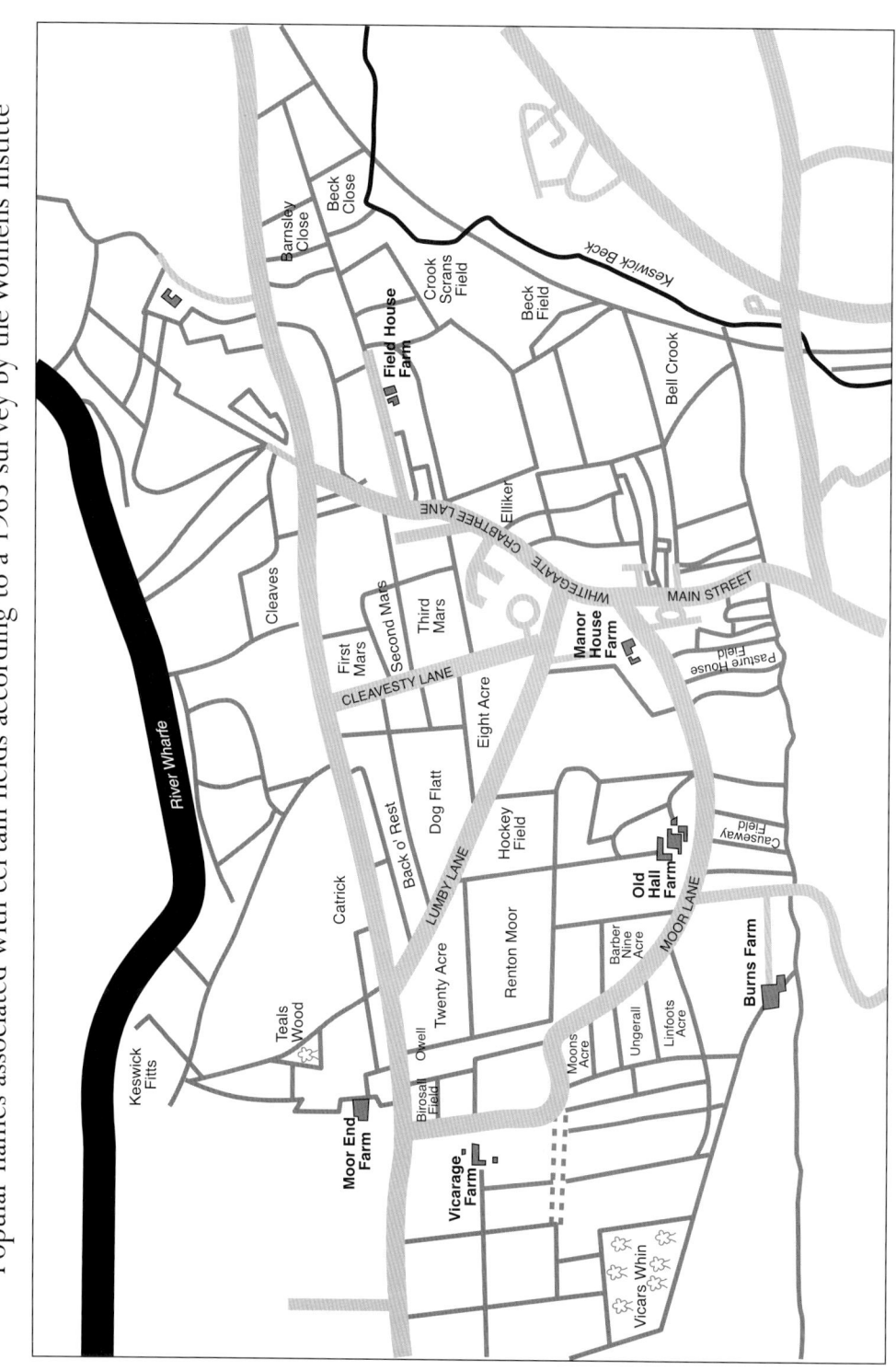

Popular names associated with certain fields according to a 1965 survey by the Womens Institute

small parcels of land, which were privately owned. For instance, in 1711, Timothy Harrison, a yeoman of East Keswick, owned 1½ acres of meadow in the Fitts and half an acre of meadow in the Bell Crook.

New Close, also known as Ox Close, was different in that Lord Harewood had manorial rights to the land. Although it was described as common pasture it contained amounts of woodland - a vital resource in the economy of East Keswick. There is also a reference in a 1726 deed to a fourth stinted pasture called Cleves Close but by 1796 it is referred to as Cleaves Wood, approximately one acre, belonging to Lord Harewood.

In the eighteenth century the right to graze animals on the Common Pastures was an asset that was bought and sold in the same way as a field or strip of land. The grazing rights were measured in terms of 'beastgates'. A beastgate entitled a farmer to graze animals, the numbers being determined by the manorial court. It was common practice, when describing grazing rights, to equate different types of livestock on the basis of animal units. This was often done in great detail; for example, in 1744, one beastgate in the Fitts and New Close equated to eight lambs or five single sheep or a three-year old heifer. In 1743 three East Keswick farmers were fined 'for putting more Good than their Stint into East Keswick Fitts Fogg' and in 1747 James Harrison of East Keswick was fined sixpence for overgrazing the Fitts.

Some records mention the ownership of beastgates in Average (or Averige), Edish and Fogg time. All of these terms have the same meaning, referring to the right to graze animals during the winter months. The manorial courts also regulated the times that the grazing could take place. In 1796 grazing was allowed in the Fitts and Bell Crook from September until March 10th. All these regulations were designed to protect the pastures from overgrazing. In 1796, however, the Township surveyor described a large tract of meadow ground, possibly referring to Bell Crook, as very much neglected and 'choked' with springs, consisting only of rushes and tufts of sour grass.

Enclosed land

The term 'enclosed/inclosed field' refers to a field with hedged, walled or fenced boundaries, in private ownership over which there were no common rights. Enclosure in the eighteenth century was the process by which either all or part of the waste or common land was fenced off into fields and cultivated; it could also refer to the division of land in the open fields into smaller hedged fields. In both instances the fields were allocated to individual owners with all rights in the land being invested in that owner.

As can be seen from the map on page 38, the areas of enclosed fields, amounting to almost half the Township in the eighteenth century, were concentrated behind the houses in the village, along the banks of Keswick Beck and overlooking the River Wharfe in the western half of the Township. Interestingly, the fields behind the houses lying on the south side of Moor Lane show a distinctive long narrow pattern possibly relating to village development around the end of the first millennium. This is in contrast with the very small, irregularly shaped fields in the area to the east of the village.

The East Keswick map of 1801 indicates several 'old inclosures', showing either the entire field or where these fields bordered onto open land. When a sizeable amount of land came under the ownership of one individual it was often informally agreed that a hedge could be planted round the blocks of strips. Examples of this can be seen on the nineteenth century maps with the typical curved boundary hedges of two of Lord Harewood's old inclosures in West Field. Such enclosure occurred over the centuries in a piecemeal fashion. A deed of 1783 mentions an inclosure of arable ground, measuring $1^{1}/_{2}$ acres, formerly taken off Beck Field. This is the only reference to the enclosure of open field land in the eighteenth century deeds, suggesting that the 'old inclosures' pre-dated 1700.

Very little land was taken into cultivation from East Keswick Common in the eighteenth century; it was surveyed as 305 acres in 1738 and 1796. However a deed of 1712 mentions 'one close … lately taken from the Common'. The 1796 survey mentions a stone thatch house and garden taken from the waste and a blacksmith's shop built on the waste.

In his valuation of the East Keswick Estate in 1797, John Ingham gave details of the crops growing in the Township's 193 enclosed fields. Thomas Bradley, for example, had 30 acres of enclosed land in 14 plots: 7 ac of oats, 6 ac barley, 4 ac barley and wheat, 5 ac fallow and the rest meadow and pasture.

East Keswick Common

The Common, a feature of the mediaeval farming scene, was still an integral part of the farming economy in East Keswick in the eighteenth century. Situated on the western side of the village on the least fertile land, it comprised one quarter of the Township's acreage.

The Common was primarily used for grazing animals. There is no mention of the right to turf for fuel on East Keswick Common though it appears there was a right to lead

Position of the boundary between East Keswick Common and West Field

'tillage' off the Common. In 1760 twenty-one villagers were grazing 576 sheep on the Common. In the absence of archival evidence it is not known which villagers had the right to use the Common, though the most likely assumption would be the ownership of a 'messuage with appurtenances'. Messuage was a term signifying a dwelling house and the surrounding property, while appurtenances referred to certain rights attaching to the property which are unspecified in the deeds. In practice it was the owner-occupiers and tenants of these properties who had rights to the Common.

The Commons of Harewood and East Keswick were conterminous but, in contrast with Harewood, whose Common virtually disappeared in the eighteenth century, East Keswick Common survived intact till the very end of the century.

In 1739 the executors of John Boulter's estate inclosed 650 acres of Harewood Common leaving about 100 acres for a 'stray' onto Keswick Common. Six or eight years after this, in the 1740s, the remainder was inclosed by Mr Lascelles, 'excepting about thirty acres, which now lyeth out in Common adjoyning Keswick Common.' The enclosure was not universally popular. At Harewood Manorial Court in 1739 it was ordered that 'no person or persons whatsoever do at any time hereafter pull down or destroy any of the fences or hedges upon any part of the new inclosures upon Harwood Common or make any way through any of them except the common way', on pain of ten shillings. This pain was repeated again in 1742.

Although the 1738/9 survey of Harewood Estate noted that '270 acres of [East Keswick Common] may be inclosed at the charge of the renter at 8s an acre' there was no enclosure of the Common for another sixty years.

Though Lord Harewood became embroiled in disputes over enclosures elsewhere on his estate he made no active attempt to enclose East Keswick Common. In 1786 there were 'divers complaints' about Lord Harewood threatening to throw down Sowden's late inclosures in Alwoodley and encouraging two men to get land within Alwoodley Waste.

In 1750 one East Keswick resident, William Teal, was involved in a legal dispute with a neighbouring landed estate over commoners' rights. James Nelthorpe, Esq. hired Teal to fetch a cartload of coals from his mines at Seacroft, which involved going across the moor or waste of Winmoor. For several years Sir Edward Gascoigne of Parlington had been demanding a toll from all carriages passing over the moor 'which is looked upon to be an oppression to the country who hath occasion to pass over the same moor with coals or other goods.' Acting on Nelthorpe's instructions, Teal refused to pay the toll of one penny demanded by James Catton, steward to Gascoigne, whereupon Catton took a pair of blinkers from one of the horse's heads as a satisfaction for such toll. Teal started a lawsuit in order to test the legality of the toll and was paid £100 by Nelthorpe for his effort. The outcome of the case is not known.

The villagers were protective of their right to graze animals on East Keswick Common, taking legal advice in 1759 when their grazing rights were threatened by overstocking by farmers from Harewood.

> 'East Keswick Common adjoyning Harewood Common divided by a rill of water, for time out of mind had a free stray of all sorts of cattle onto Harewood Common and Harewood likewise onto Keswick Common…Now these several years [since the enclosure of Harewood Common] the tennants in Harewood hath turned out Great Numbers of Cattle onto the aforesd stray or stripe of land adjoyning East Keswick Common, which is about 30 acres, and East Keswick Common being about 300 acres, whereby the stocks of cattle belonging to Harewood is seemingly greater than the stock of cattle belonging East Keswick, on the Common of East Keswick to yhe great oppression of the sd common.'

The legal opinion was that the Commoners of Harewood had no entitlement to East Keswick Common; 'The Commoners of Harewood having inclosed the greatest part of their Common cannot put more beasts upon their Common than the part yet remaining unenclosed can maintain.' When asked if East Keswick could make a fence against Harewood Common or keep a herdsman to tent the said Common, Jno Stanhope was of the opinion that without the Lord's consent the Commoners could do neither. In 1760 the dispute was still unresolved, with the Harewood Commoners grazing 487 sheep on the Common.

It seems there was no interest in the village to enclose and divide up the Common. In 1783 James Teal, when valuing the property of William Teal in East Keswick, commented,

> 'The Common Right upon an inclosure it is supposed upon a moderate computation would be worth £60 but as an inclosure is not thought of at present the same is only valued at half that sum.'

Relations between Landlord and Tenant Farmer

When Henry Lascelles bought his first property in East Keswick in 1739 four of the tenants were in arrears. Holmes owed £45-10s and was allowed to pay £30 and the remainder was 'abated'. Similarly Hodgson was released from paying all his back rent as he was a poor man and not able to pay. Arrears became more numerous in the 1750s and early 1760s, possibly connected with the cattle plague that swept the country in the mid eighteenth century. There were no further arrears from 1765 to the end of the century. Although the surveyor of Harewood Estate in 1738 considered the rents to be low, they remained unchanged for the next sixty years. In 1797, following a review of the tenancies, the rents were increased, in many cases doubled, and increased again substantially in 1799. In three years the total rents had increased from £334 to £899. There were no formal complaints about the rent increases nor did the rent increases in the 1790s cause any of the East Keswick tenants to leave their farms. The fact that the rents had remained very low in the eighteenth century and that agriculture was enjoying a boom time during the Napoleonic Wars may have reconciled the tenants to the rent increases. The rents then remained at the 1799 level until at least 1811.

Although the number of freeholders fell in the course of the eighteenth century, as Lascelles bought up the estates, in most cases they were not owner-occupiers - many of the landlords lived at a distance. There is no record as to whether tenants favoured the accessibility of the new landlord and his agent or the remoteness of the absentee landlord.

Generally the sitting tenant remained tenant of the newly acquired property. It is interesting to note that in 1755, Isaac Bailey, a tenant farmer in East Keswick, wrote to

Edwin Lascelles in London rather than to his agent at Harewood, requesting an urgent settlement of his tenancy,

> 'I have prevailed with Mr Bunny to part with the land for £260....but I was obliged to go over to him, before I could get him to consent. I hope your Honr remembers, that I was promis'd to have that house and premises, which yr Honr purchased of Mr Midgley, and, in relying upon that promise, I have agreed to give up the house I now live in....as for the land belonging to it, I have given it up already.....I most humbly request that yr honr would please to permit me to rent ...Midgley Farm...to enter now, otherwise I shall not know what to do with my stock of cattle'.

Correspondence between Edwin Lascelles in London and his agent at Harewood reveals the extent to which Lascelles involved himself in the minutiae of estate management, all the more remarkable given the total size of the Harewood Estates and Lascelles' involvement in other business and political affairs. In 1755 he wrote a lengthy letter concerning the morals and character of a local publican 'Old Brewerton'.

> 'I forgot to ...reprimand him for keeping a bawdy house but assure him from me that [if he continue] in his vile and wicked practices he shall be turned out of his house...and also make it known to the strumpets his daughters that they shall be sent to the House of Correction if they continue to play the Prostitutes...The two harlots and the Old Pimp the Father are enough to ruin all the young fellows in the Town.'

Interestingly, nearly half a century later, a Henry Brewerton owned a brewhouse in East Keswick - was he a descendant of 'Old Brewerton'?

5

The Enclosure Act changes all

In the second half of the eighteenth century the rate of land enclosure in England accelerated as townships and parishes obtained their own Private Acts of Parliament to enable enclosure to take place. Six million acres of common and open field land were enclosed, mostly in the period 1760 to 1830.

After 1792 the Lascelles family owned more than half the property in East Keswick and was therefore in a strong position locally to press for enclosure. On the death of Edwin Lascelles in 1795, his cousin and heir Edward Lascelles, who took a seat in the House of Lords in 1797, was able to use his political influence in London to instigate Parliamentary enclosure of East Keswick Common and Open Fields.

In 1796 a survey was made of all the Harewood properties. The surveyor urged enclosure in East Keswick as it 'would embrace a large tract of uncultivated common upwards of 300 acres now of little or no use but which would then be worth in many parts more than a guinea an acre.' He contested that the common fields would similarly benefit from enclosure and that more than twice the present produce would be reaped, but that this could not be done to any effect while so many people were interested in the same field. He was echoing the opinions and propaganda of agriculturists of the day and the justifications given in thousands of petitions to Parliament to enclose common land and the open fields.

In October 1796 a notice appeared in *The Leeds Intelligencer* concerning 'Harewood, East Keswick and Weardley Intended Inclosures'. Owners were requested to meet at the house of Mr John Greaves, innkeeper at Harewood, to consider an application to be made to Parliament to obtain an Act. They formally petitioned Parliament for leave to bring in a Bill on the premise that the 'open fields [and] commons, are not, in their present situation, capable of improvement, nor can be occupied to such advantage as they might be if the same were divided and inclosed…' Mr Henry Lascelles MP [son of Edward, 1st Earl of Harewood] presented the Bill on February 17th 1797. There was no opposition to the Inclosure Bill in Parliament; the Committee noted that all parties concerned had given their consent, except the Trustees of land belonging to Leeds Charity School, who could not be met with. By March 2nd it had passed the Commons, a week later the Lords agreed to the Bill without amendment and on the 10th it received Royal Assent.

In general terms the Act for East Keswick and Harewood followed the same format as thousands of other Parliamentary Acts of the time. In allotting the 690 acres of land the Commissioners were to observe the following conditions -

Firstly, Lord Harewood was to be allocated $1/16$th of the total land acreage 'as a compensation for his Right and Interest in and to the soil of the said moors or commons so intended to be inclosed…'

The Vicar of Harewood was then entitled to an acreage equalling $1/7$th of the remaining common lands and $1/7$th of the ancient inclosed lands.

Only after these allocations was the remaining land to be divided amongst the owners in proportion to the yearly value of their common right.

Lord Harewood was sufficiently influential to demand an entitlement to New Close and that part of the Commons on each side of the Turnpike road, ranging in a line with the outsides of the clumps of trees (these avenues of trees remain today).

The Enclosure Award

The Enclosure Award, dated January 6th 1801, is a lengthy document that sets out in detail information about the new allotments, ditches and hedges and the specifications of the roads adjacent to the land being enclosed. Accompanying the Award was a map that shows the roads and fields referred to in the Award. For each of the 177 fields the Award gives the owner's name and the acreage and describes the position by reference to the field it was in and the number on the map. It details the ownership of lands on its boundaries and allocates responsibility for the maintenance of the boundaries. The Award also detailed the location and widths of 21 public and private carriageways, bridleways and footpaths.

Prospective road makers were to attend a meeting at Harewood in May 1799 where the Commissioners would let the construction of the new roads in East Keswick. In October 1801 the surveyor informed the Justices of Peace that the roads were finished and ready for the passage of travellers and carriages. In December 1798 the Harewood Estate paid £5-10s for quickwood for the enclosure hedges. In 1799 and 1800 a total of £184 was paid for ditching the newly enclosed common and fields.

The Effects of Enclosure in East Keswick

One of the debates in agricultural history has centred round the impact of enclosures on the small farmer and the rural poor. Even at the time of the parliamentary enclosures there was disagreement over the extent of dispossession in rural areas. It was claimed that the commoners, people with rights to the common, were turned into labourers and that the substitution of small plots of land did not compensate for the loss of their rights. Certainly the gains made by the smaller owners, totalling 60 acres, appear insignificant when compared with the 126 acres granted to Lord Harewood and 113 acres allocated to the Church. The extra acreage also involved the additional costs of hedging and ditching and, in some instances, the loss of grazing rights. However the records suggest that few of the rural poor in East Keswick had Commoners' rights. Moreover the number of freeholders in East Keswick had been declining for many years before Enclosure and there is no evidence that Enclosure accelerated the process.

There is no direct reference in the records of the effects of enclosure on East Keswick. However this cannot be taken as proof of the benign consequences of enclosure since records tend to revolve round the more substantial members of society or round events involving large numbers of people. The effects of enclosure on a relatively few people in a village did not constitute a sufficiently large statistical group to impact on the authors of the various records. Then, as now, it is difficult to disentangle personal circumstances from wider socio-economic trends - and more so in the context of one village. It is impossible to know just how far the effects of enclosure as exemplified in a newspaper article of 1798 were typical of the experience of rural labourers.

> 'About 33 years ago, in consequence of the inclosure at Poppleton [Mr Britton Abbot] was under the necessity, with six helpless children, and his wife nearly downlying, of quitting a comfortable habitation.'

His enterprise in applying for some land by the roadside near Tadcaster and building a house there was commended by the newspaper -

> 'How much more animated and grateful would be the view of picturesque villages, let on very small rents to useful members of society, around a park, than those useless uninhabited and uninhabitable pigmy models of Grecian Temples and Gothic Castles which a perverted taste has rendered so numerous.'

It has been suggested that the census returns for 1801 and 1811 for East Keswick, as printed in abstract form in 1831, are evidence of a significant drop in population at the time of the enclosure. The figures show a total population fall from 535 to 267, with a similar marked reduction in the number of houses from 98 to 61. There were 61 houses in 1821, with a population of 296. However no other evidence supported the dramatic fall in population. The number of births in the years 1790-1811 remained fairly constant. A comparison of the 1801 and 1851 maps showed no obvious loss of housing stock. No other village in Yorkshire, even those which had enclosed in this period, showed depopulation on the scale of East Keswick. It appears that the discrepancy was a result of statistical error. Teal, in his early nineteenth century scrapbook, included the 'Answers to questions contained in the Schedule to an Act 1801 Population for East Keswick'. This showed there were 61 families in East Keswick and 44 houses with a total population of 234.

In general the records suggest that the Enclosure marked no great watershed in the lives of the agricultural population of East Keswick.

Tithes in East Keswick

The tithes supported the Rector of a parish. From the time of the Reformation in the sixteenth century about a third of all tithes came to be owned by lay people. Originally tithes were paid in kind - a tenth of all produce. The great tithes were of corn and hay, the small tithes of livestock, wool and non-cereal crops. In some parishes the landowners paid a fixed sum of money, known as a modus, replacing the tithe in kind. In 1724 Lady Elizabeth Hastings, who owned the tithes of East Keswick, agreed to settle the Great Tithes on the Vicar of Harewood and his successors, yielding £37 a year. A Terrier of 1764 (listing the church's assets in the parish) mentions 'All Tythes, great and small, within the Township of East Keswick (except a Modus for the Tythe Hay) given by the late Lady Elizabeth Hastings.'

It was quite a common occurrence for the enclosure acts to allot land to the tithe owners in lieu of tithe as it eliminated sources of dispute between the church and landowners. This appears to have been the case in East Keswick. The surveyor of East Keswick in 1797 noted 'The present Incumbent of Harewood however the Reverend Tattersall has thought it proper to dispute the Right of Modus but there is not the smallest shadow of evidence for him to claim upon - added to which many of the tenants have receipts from the old Incumbents specifying a certain Modus being paid in lieu of Tithe Hay.' As a result the church was granted 165 acres of land at the time of enclosure and no Tithe Award or map was made for East Keswick, consequent upon the Tithe Commutation Act of 1836.

A new farming landscape

The beginning of the nineteenth century marked the end of hundreds of years of farming the open fields and grazing the common and open pastures.

A substantial number of the farm properties on the Harewood Estate in East Keswick were in a bad state of repair in 1799. The Harewood Estate Account Book 1806-35 mentions certain improvements in East Keswick though not on the scale of farm building in some other villages. Reference is made to new flags costing £5-8-8d at Benjamin Clough's house in 1806, the sinking of a well at John Clough's new farm in 1814, the building of several new cottages in East Keswick in 1820 and several new buildings on three of the farms. The 1840s survey mentions an outlay of between £400-500 spent on new buildings on John Scatchard's holding.

In 1832 mention was made of payment for 84,000 draining tiles and 100,000 bricks for the improvement of the Estate. However in 1847 the Estate auditor observed that many parts of the Yorkshire Estate were capable of great improvement in drainage. It is clear that East Keswick was included in this observation. In a memorandum on the subject of Keswick Drain the auditor wrote -

> '...It will drain a good extent of land much in need of it when complete, but the tenants do not seem disposed to improve the surface to the extent they might.'

No doubt the financial implications of such undertakings were a major consideration in the tenants' reluctance. In 1850 it was noted - 'Farmers universally complaining ...that they are losing money.'

It would appear that the marked slump in agricultural prices in the late 1840s and early 1850s affected the degree to which Harewood Estate felt it could exert pressure on its

An early twentieth century photograph of harvesting on an East Keswick farm

tenants to make improvements. In the late 1840s some tenants were given notice to quit having been found coursing hares with a cur dog; however the notice was withdrawn as 'the farm would be difficult to let.'

In 1848 Mr Teale, who rented a good cottage and 36 acres in East Keswick for £50 a year, was under notice to quit because of persistent rent arrears, despite a rent reduction of £20 five years earlier. Although Teale sold some land to pay off most of the arrears the Steward saw 'no hope of his doing any good by being allowed to go on'. However several considerations swayed the decision to allow Teale to remain. His brother-in-law, who was 'a respectable man' and had a large livery in Leeds (providing potential manure for the land), took responsibility for the holding. It was pointed out that, as Teale and his family had been Harewood tenants for many years and he had five children, it would be probable his Lordship would feel under the necessity of giving him employment or doing something towards his support.

A similar mixture of paternalistic concern and consideration of the financial management of the Estate was evinced in the case of Joseph Hardcastle, who had been a tenant of Harewood property since 1803. In 1819 he was £10 in arrears. At this time the Trustees of the Cutler- Boulter Almshouses in Oxford had a vacancy for a poor man of Harewood Parish, who should be single, sober, of good moral character, a member of the established church and regularly attend divine service on the Lord's Day. The Harewood agent Mr Menzies proposed Mr Hardcastle. This brought him into conflict with the Vicar, Richard Hale, who would not agree to nominate Hardcastle, as he had not seen him in the Parish Church for ten years. However Hale seemed to recognise his inability to influence the decision, conceding that Menzies would only do what he wanted.

In 1847, Mr W Midgley, formerly of East Keswick, gave notice to quit his tenancy of Rufforth Grange after only three years unless £30 was taken off the rent - the 'Rent being too high' - £260 for 219 acres. The agent noted that Midgley 'is the sort of tenant to keep if possible'; the reason given was that he had landed property of his own in East Keswick and was well off for capital.

Farms were increasingly let to farmers from outside East Keswick from the mid nineteenth century onwards. The large number of letters applying for Harewood Estate farms in the early years of the twentieth century indicates the distances some applicants were prepared to travel.

The rental agreements drawn up between Lord Harewood and his tenants specified the methods of husbandry and reflect the importance attached to the maintenance and improvement of soil fertility. The following is an extract from an agreement between the Harewood Estate and William Teal, yeoman of East Keswick, for the letting of 25 acres in 1796.

> '...he will keep and leave all the buildings, gates, stiles, hedges, and drains, in a good state of repair. That he will do his utmost to preserve and nurse up all the young timber he possibly can, and not cut, maim, or prune any maiden tree upon the premises...That he will drain all wet parts of the farm by the best and most complete methods. That he will spend and consume all the hay, straw...upon the premises to the best advantage That he will not break up any meadow or pasture, which has been laid more than ten years, without licence first... That he will not sow any of the arable land, with teasels, woad, hemp, or flax, without leave. That he will strictly observe one of the following rules of cropping his arable lands. Viz. If he uses it in a three-course shift, to have one full third part of the whole every year, in a clean whole year summer fallow. And in case he uses it in a four course shift, that not more than one half shall be sown with corn, grain, or pulse, in any one year, the other half to be either in turnips, vetches, clover, or some other grass seeds, to be eaten off upon the premises for the purpose of enriching the land...'

On taking the tenancy of Old Hall Farm in 1841 John Johnson agreed to

> 'manage the said farm according to the best Methods of Husbandry
>
> not to take from the Arable lands more than two crops of corn in succession without a summer fallow, or a turnip fallow
>
> to spread not less than eight well filled cart horse loads of good rotten manure, or three chaldrons of Lime upon every acre of fallow
>
> to manure the old meadow lands at a rate of 8 cart loads per acre every 2 years
>
> from time to time yearly spread upon the lands all the compost, dung, ashes and manure which shall arise upon the premises'

In marked contrast with the present day, East Keswick would be alive with the presence of people working on the farms and in the fields. However, like servants below the stairs, the huge army of agricultural workers receives scant attention in the records. They are mentioned in passing in the records relating to the relief of poverty and their occupations are mentioned in the census returns 1851-91 and occasionally in the parish registers. While there are difficulties in using the census returns for a direct comparison of the labour force in the second half of the nineteenth century, they nevertheless provide a name, age and place of birth to people who would otherwise be statistics.

The agricultural workforce consisted of family members, farm servants, labourers and casual and part-time workers. The farm servants lived at the farm, employed on an annual basis, while the agricultural labourers generally lived in the village, employed on a weekly or daily basis. A number of permanent workers would live in tied houses; the 1796 survey of East Keswick shows several farmers renting cottages. The formal written agreement between William Teal, lime burner of East Keswick, and three of his workers illustrates the way many farmers and farm workers combined agricultural work with other jobs.

> 'Robert Manners and Benjamin Ellison of East Keswick and John Massey of Collingham were to get 140 kilns of limestones and wheel them to the kiln sides…to assist William Teal in setting the kilns as often as William Teal shall require them
>
> The three to assist William Teal with his hay time and harvest if required according to the custom of the township of East Keswick.'

In 1867, the Harewood land agent reported:

> 'the cottages in the area are substantial and clean, but many are not very convenient in the upper floors, having sleeping roofs and ventilation. There is generally one sitting room, bedroom, and pantry below, and two bedrooms above, and the average rent is 1s a week. [NB the ordinary rate of pay at this time was 14s a week] Cottages are frequently, when let with the farms, sublet by [the farmers] to persons not being their own labourers, and at a rent higher than what other labourers are paying.'

Until the 1911 census returns become available it is not possible to locate the houses of the agricultural workers in East Keswick. However it is likely they occupied the lowest rated properties, all of which were rented. For example, there was a concentration of low rated houses on the east side of Main Street opposite Lumby Lane, seven of which were described as old stone built, with a room, kitchen, two bedrooms with a privy or closet in the yard. By the mid twentieth century East Keswick, in common with other West Riding villages, had a supply of council housing available for farm workers.

The second group of farm workers was the Farm Servants, who lived in - hence the mention of a second staircase in several of the farmhouse descriptions in 1910. They were hired for a year at the 'statute fairs ' in November. Several of the farm servants were born in East Keswick - given the size of Victorian families and the cottages it is unsurprising that the older children moved out as soon as they reached working age.

Between 1851 and 1891 the number of agricultural labourers fell from 46 to 26; the total agricultural workforce, including labourers, male farm servants and family members fell from 62 to 44 in the same period. In 1867 it was reported that 'Labour is not abundant owing to the proximity to manufacturing towns, which draw off young men at a rate of wages higher than is paid for agricultural work.' Only a history of East Keswick families would reveal the extent to which this was true.

Apparently conflicting evidence was given in 1867 concerning the use of female and child labour no doubt reflecting the different social status of the larger farmers and the smallholders/ farm workers.

> 'it is a very rare thing for women and children to be employed in field work in this district. The women will not go out to work even to charring. No boys under 14 go to the field.'

some small holders 'employ no Labourers but work the farms by themselves and their children.'

Certainly the school records confirm that even later in the century and into the twentieth century children were often absent from school to work on the farms.

In 1867 it was reported that much of the labour in the area was supplied by the Irish. In 1861 six Irish farm labourers were lodging in two houses in East Keswick. In the twentieth century the Dalby family can remember itinerant Irish workers lodging in the barn at Manor Farm. In the twentieth century gangs of 'Bramham women' came to the East Keswick farms potato-picking. In the Second World War German, Italian, Russian and Polish prisoners of war were allocated to the farms.

6

Farms, smallholdings and nurseries

It is difficult to extrapolate trends in farming at a village level, despite the apparent wealth of detailed and diverse source material in the nineteenth and twentieth centuries. Without a series of rent accounts for the Harewood property, similar to that for the eighteenth century, a study of the number and size of holdings derives mainly from three surveys of Harewood Estate property in East Keswick, dated c.1843, 1872 (updated 1886) and 1927.

The first detailed information about farmers of non-Harewood property after the 1796 survey was not until 1943.

The location of farms in the nineteenth century is not as straightforward as it would appear. There are no surviving maps of Harewood holdings in East Keswick before 1886. Directories and census returns only occasionally mention the name of the farm and the Ordnance Survey maps do not name the smaller farms. Moreover the similarity of farm names can cause problems when trying to marry farm names with specific properties. For example Moor Farm could refer to Keswick Moor Farm or Moor End Farm. In 1801 Moor End Farm was next to East Keswick Beck; later in the century it was the name given to the farm along Harewood Avenue. Keswick Field Farm later became Field House Farm. One of the farms was variously known as Keswick Moor Farm and Farfield House, not to be confused with a farm further up Harewood Avenue called Farfield Farm.

Since 1800 farming in East Keswick has become more and more concentrated in the hands of the larger farmers and the number and size of the smaller farms has contracted.

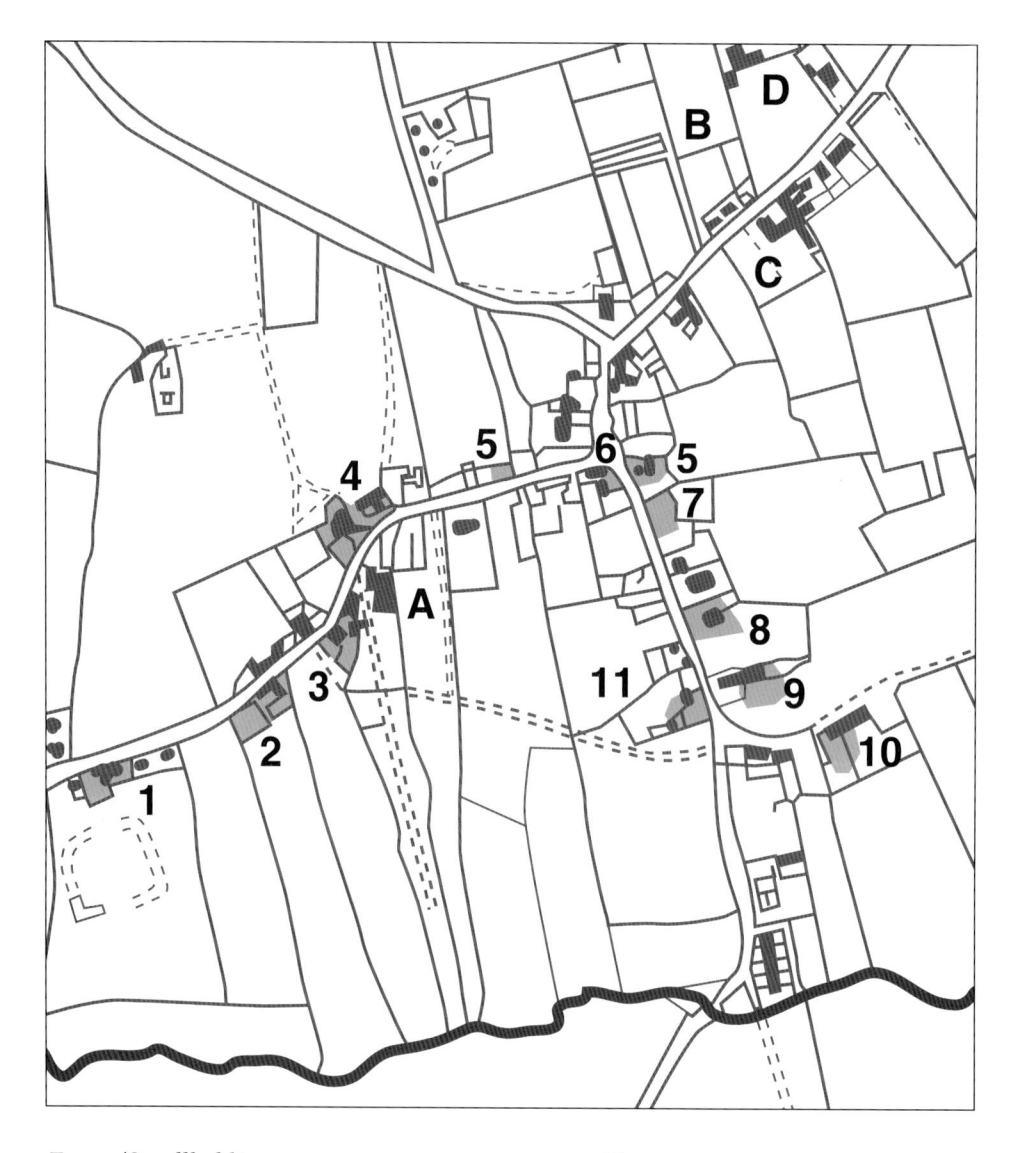

Farms/Smallholdings

1. Moat House Farm
2. Ivy Grange farm
3. Pasture House Farm
4. Manor Farm
5. Stocks Hill Farm house and buildings
6. North View
7. Argyle House
8. Jessamine Cottage
9. South View
10. Clitheroe House
11. Darley House

Nurseries

A. Valley Gardens
B. Whitegates (Duthoits)
C. Ashfield Nurseries
D. Rose Nurseries

Market gardening and nurseries became an increasingly important aspect of rural life in East Keswick from the 1870s.

Mrs Brierley recollects that in the 1920s the village was a little farming community, where you knew everyone and when they passed you they always spoke. People living in the newly constructed Allerton Drive were newcomers and regarded as a world apart from the village.

> 'There weren't tractors that went up and down the village. There were horses and carts and ponies and traps and the odd few people had bicycles and they were really up in the world.'

This chapter looks in more detail at the individual farms, smallholdings and market gardens in East Keswick during the period 1870s -1970s.

Farms

Manor Farm

Manor Farm, like all the farms in the village, had fields that were dispersed. This was in contrast with the ring-fenced farms situated outside the village, created from the enclosure of the open fields and common. In 1871 John Parker, born in East Keswick, farmed 148 acres at Manor Farm. By 1886 the farm was 164 acres, having gained several fields from the dispersal of two smallholdings. In 1922 John James Dalby took over the tenancy from the Burnett family. He had previously been a tenant farmer at Fortshot House in Wike. The Dalby family has farmed Manor Farm to the present day and has other farms in the district.

In 1915 the farm was described as follows:

> 'lumber room with loft above, stable for 4 and barn and wheelhouse, implement shed (part wood), stable for 2, mistal for 4, hay and turnip house (stone slated) mistal for 23, 2 boxes and mistal for 5. Old house in ruins, box, mistal for 4 and shed. Washhouse and old cottage used as shed.'

Manor Farm

In 1950, when the farm was sold to Mr Dalby, the description of the farm buildings reflected the changes brought about by increasing mechanisation of farm work and developments in animal husbandry.

> '3 poultry houses, barn, workshop, loose box with granary over, dairy, cooling place with tiled walls, cowhouse for 4, fodder house (electric power), large cowhouse with concrete divisions for 34 (re-roofed recently), 7-bay Dutch barn erected by tenant, 2 poultry houses and pig sty, small covered fold.'

In the 1960s the Dalbys had a retail milk round in the village, using milk from their other farms. They had a herd of beef cattle, a flock of sheep, twenty pigs (gone by 1977) and hens at Manor Farm.

Old Hall Farm

In 1841 John Johnson of Alwoodley, aged only about 24, took the tenancy of Old Hall Farm, known as 'John Sharper Clough Farm', amounting to 105 acres. He farmed there for over fifty years. Some land near the Wharfe, part of a former smallholding, was added to the farm between 1886 and 1915.

Edmund Johnson was farming the 123-acre holding in 1915, when the land near the house was described as good, but that nearer the moor as poorer and of a rough nature. Edmund retired in 1919 and the farm was taken by the Carters. The Scott family took over the tenancy of the farm in about 1925. In the 1930s the farm had a retail milk round, delivered by the farm man on a bike. In 1944 H Scott and JD Carter, both of Old Hall Farm, were applying to Lord Harewood for smaller holdings in the village. By 1950 the farm was let to Mr Dalby and at the time of its sale (to the tenant) the farm was only 41 acres.

In 1915 the farm buildings included a stable, two mistals, a shed, a turnip house and calf boxes and barn, all stone built, flagged and in good repair. Eighty years later Mrs Brierley can still remember the names of the three horses on Old Hall Farm - Gypsy, Jet and Jewel.

By 1950 a tractor house and two temporary implement sheds had been erected. In 1943 all the farm work was done with horses; only three farms in East Keswick had tractors at this time and even then they retained horses for agricultural purposes. Tractors quickly replaced horsepower and by 1958 there were only three agricultural horses left in the village.

Field House Farm

In 1833 Thomas and Jonathon Midgley took the tenancy of this 110-acre farm on the death of William Marston. In 1812 there was mention of a 'new farm' of 89 acres for William Marston the Elder and his son.

Charles Buckborough, born in East Keswick, was farming Field House Farm from at least 1851 to 1871. Members of the Midgley family, who were related by marriage to Buckborough, were farming there into the 1920s.

The farm gained extra land by Keswick Beck when a small farm at Darley House was dispersed. By the Second World War the farm had acquired the holding belonging to Jessamine Cottage. In 1943 the farm extended to 233 acres.

The Lupton family took over the tenancy in 1927 having previously farmed at Stainburn near Otley.

The farm was primarily a dairy farm. A comparison of the buildings in 1915 and 1950 reflects the changes in dairy farming in these years.

Field House Farm

'1915   buildings all stone flagged and in good repair, 2 pig-cotes and hen houses, mistal for 10 with loft above, barn, mistal for 14, box, stable for 4 hay house and trap shed, cart shed and wheelhouse, turnip shed and implement shed (lean to).'

'1950   garage, boiler house, dairy with concrete floor, very good cowhouse for 10 with concrete floor and water laid on, 2 stall stable, open fold, meal house with electric power laid on, very good cowhouse for 14 with concrete floor, large barn with granary over, very good cowhouse for 11 with concrete floor and tubular steel divisions and water laid on, similar cowhouse for 9, small covered fold, open fronted timber built implement shed, 2-bay cartshed'

The introduction of mains electricity and water supplies, enabling machine milking and mechanisation of the milk bottling process, resulted in milk production on a much larger scale while employing the same labour force. Field House Farm and Manor Farm were the only farms in East Keswick to have electricity in the buildings by 1943.

Although most of the market gardens and smallholdings in the village had piped water by this date those farms outside the main village, Moor End Farm, Old Hall Farm, Vicarage Farm and Keswick Moor Farm, had no piped water or electricity supplies to the house or buildings.

The Luptons had a retail milk round on their 220-acre farm but sold it in the 1960s. In the 1930s the milk was delivered by bike twice a day.

Vicarage Farm

In East Keswick many boundaries between the centuries-old, small, irregular fields have been removed and larger, more regular fields have taken their place. This is illustrated by a comparison of the size of fields comprising Field House Farm in 1833 and 1950, though it should be noted that as it was a dairy farm the enlargement of fields was to a lesser extent than on arable farms. The number of fields fell from 35 to 22 and the number of fields between one and five acres fell from 27 to four. East Keswick has been fortunate in that hedge removal has been less extensive than in some areas.

The farm was sold in the late 1990s for conversion to private dwellings and the land has been split up and is farmed by farmers from Wike and Harewood.

Vicarage Farm

Mr Emsley, Mr JW Stead, Mr Dearlove and Mr GS Briggs were tenants of this farm during the first half of the twentieth century.

Keswick Moor Farm

In 1943 it was noted that it was heavy wet land and the condition of the field drainage was bad. Attempts to improve the farm were handicapped by shortage of labour during the war.

The tenant at Vicarage Farm had installed electricity by 1951 and the water came via a windmill in a nearby field.

In 1965 the 120-acre farm had a Friesian dairy herd and a retail milk business. By 1977 Mr Terry had left and the farm was amalgamated with Burns Farm to form a 230-acre holding.

Keswick Moor Farm or Farfield House

In 1861 the 105-acre farm was tenanted by Seth Elsworth, aged 29, born in Thorner. By 1881 Edward Bland, born at Newton, had taken over the tenancy. In the late 1930s Herbert Hall took over the tenancy from Fred Jackson, who in turn had taken the tenancy after WA Webster. A substantial acreage of land was added to the farm when Pasture House Farm was dispersed.

In 1915 it was noted that the 'land is fair but hilly and there are a few old quarries on it.' In 1908 Mr Moon of East Keswick required more arable land to grow corn and straw for fodder for his stock but the rabbit nuisance and the 14 acres of quarries deterred him from applying for Keswick Moor Farm.

Before and after the Second World War people from Leeds spent camping weekends and holidays on this and Field House Farm, an arrangement which was discontinued with the introduction of tighter regulations.

In the 1960s Mr Hall had pigs, sheep and a milk herd on the 200-acre farm. By 1977 a milk pipeline and bulk tank had been installed. The land is now contracted out to farmers from Spofforth.

Moor End Farm

In 1886 William Whitley farmed 56 acres at Moor End Farm. Charles Jackson, Harry Kirby, Mr Taylor, William Crossland and Arthur Rhodes were tenants from the 1890s to 1951.

Moor End Farm

In 1965 the 90-acre farm was used by Mr Smith to rear and fatten cattle, which supplied his butcher's shops. He had a herd of 60 prize winning Highland Cattle.

By 1977 Mr Hallam, a solicitor, had a herd of pedigree Galloway cattle at Moor End Farm.

Clitheroe House, Clitheroe Cottage and South View

In the 1880s Joseph Laurence, schoolmaster and farmer, rented 18 acres of land down School Lane which included Clitheroe Cottage and Clitheroe House. After his death in 1886 the holding was split up.

Clitheroe Cottage became a separate dwelling.

South View was a 17-acre smallholding farmed by Richard Johnson in 1915. In 1925 it was tenanted by the butcher Roland Illingworth.

> 'we used to buy beef cattle from Ireland …an agent used to send them by boat to Liverpool then by rail to Bardsey Station then we would walk them to East Keswick and feed them on at South View. We often used to walk them and later take them by cattle wagon to slaughter at Harewood'.

They also bought pigs, sheep and cattle at Tadcaster, Pannal and Wetherby cattle markets - all now gone!

Illingworths had two shops, at East Keswick and Harewood, and used to supply Harewood House and surrounding villages with meat, delivered by pony trap in the early days, later by bike and vans.

In the Second World War no private slaughtering was allowed and the land was sublet to a farmer at Rigton.

In 1950 South View and its land was bought by the Illingworths, whose family were butchers in East Keswick for three generations from 1910 to 1990.

After 1886 the smallholding at Clitheroe House became a separate holding. Its four fields near the Church were known as 'Barber's Land' and had belonged to a small farm on West End in the 1880s. In 1915 Clitheroe House was occupied by Joseph Linfoot. In

Haymaking on Burns Farm around 1950

1943 Clitheroe House and its 16 acres were farmed as part of Gateon House Farm in Bardsey. Mr Ridsdale remembers 'they'd bring some stock and put it on this land during the winter and let them eat it off and in summertime they'd let it grow to meadow and cut it for hay and they used to cart it back up to Gateon House.'

A Wimpey housing estate was started in the fields near the Church in the 1960s. Owing to a discrepancy in the location of the green belt on the maps at Wakefield and Wetherby it was many years before Wimpeys were allowed to build beyond the footpath to the line of the drain.

Stocks Hill

In 1886 Stocks Hill was a 9-acre smallholding in the centre of the village with several fields further away. David Parker farmed here from about 1861 to the 1890s. He was born in East Keswick and also acted as sub-postmaster.

James Bryant farmed Stocks Hill for almost fifty years from 1901. By 1915 the farmhouse was in Moor Lane (West End), separate from the farm buildings and land.

In the 1930s this was one of three smallholdings in the village selling milk. Mr Bryant milked six cows by hand and delivered the milk in cans round the village. He had a notice board in his garden 'Milk and Cream for Sale'.

The smallholders bought in straw but made their own hay. Mr Derek Illingworth recalls:

> 'I helped them all as a lad. They used to get another fellow to cut it and four or five of us would make it and lead it home, just loose - forkfuls of hay - and make a stack in the yard. There were no bales in those days.'

> 'In summer Mr. Bryant used to take his cows, what they call tenting on the roadside. He used to go and sit with his milking stool and his paper and his five or six cows would be eating the grass on the roadside and they used to go a bit further every day.'

In 1909 Mr Bryant advertised as a carting agent: 'Furniture Removed, Pony and Trap for Hire'. 'He used to take his horse and cart and go up to Bardsey Station, fill the cart with a ton of coal, bring it back and drop it off at your gate or door, and that was a pound.'

On one occasion, while delivering a load to Mr Wormald's above The Parsonage, a terrific thunderstorm washed all the coal down the village to the Duke of Wellington!

North View

The Allenby family farmed this 6-acre smallholding from at least the early 1840s to the 1870s. As the property had pig cotes, sheds, cow houses and a fold yard it is possible that they rented additional land. In 1881 John Watson, a farmer, coal dealer and carter, lived here. In 1909 he was hiring out 'Landau, Waggonette and Pony Trap'. In the 1920s Mr Watson did a lot of carting work. Like Mr Bryant he carted coals round the village and had a small milk round, delivered in cans by the family.

Mr Illingworth recalls that in the 1930s

> 'Mr Aubrey Watson used to make hay for Mr Bryant. He had horses and a reaper and a wagon to cart it home. Mr Bryant hadn't any implements. We had because we had a small farm at Harewood…We went along Harewood Avenue with a horse and cart to make hay here.'

In 1941, Mr Aubrey Watson farmed 19 ½ acres. At the time of the sale Bryants rented the 11-acre holding.

In 1973 land, known as Watson's Garth, was sold to build four detached houses.

Ivy Grange/House/Cottage

William Wright, born in East Keswick, was farming this 30-acre holding from at least 1841 to 1861, when he was 82. His son Thomas lived on the farm, taking it over after his father's death. After William's death in the 1890s the farm size remained the same and was occupied by Thomas Barber, the local pig-killer, for several decades. In 1915 the farm had stabling with loft above, a cowhouse for seven with a loft above, a barn, shed and calf box, all stone and flagged and in fair repair.

By the Second World War the smallholding was less than five acres.

Argyle House

The Midgley family owned several farms in East Keswick but in the early years of the twentieth century they were sold off. For example, the property between the parsonage and Lumby Lane had been a farm. By 1915 it was a private residence but there were still redundant farm buildings in the yard in the 1930s. Only one of the Midgley properties survived as a smallholding. Their other land in the village was sold for market gardening or as building land. In 1907 Hedley Wright bought the farm with a cottage known as Barn House and a butcher's shop and slaughterhouse. In 1915 the property had an old tiled cow house for four. Mr Illingworth can remember as a boy, in the 1930s, going with a can to collect milk from the farmhouse. William Mulrooney, a part-time farmer and haulage contractor, started to farm at Argyle House in about 1935/36. He had a small dairy herd on the 14-acre smallholding but did not sell the milk direct to the public. In the early 1950s the property was sold to J Revis, who had a haulage business here. He took one crop off the land then sold it for housing; 'The Close' was built on it.

Jessamine Cottage

In 1886 Jessamine Cottage was a 20-acre smallholding, rented by Joshua Barrett, a farmer and butcher. His father, William, was a farmer, innkeeper and butcher in East Keswick in 1851.

James Harland, also a farmer and butcher, took over the farm in the mid 1890s. In 1915 the buildings were described as 'very old!' The fields were some distance from the farm, by Keswick Beck and across the main road behind The Star. Bramham Moor Hunt used to meet in one of these fields off Main Street.

In 1927 the farm was incorporated into Field House Farm and bought by Luptons in the 1950 sale. It was used to house bought-in cattle until they were tuberculin-tested and could join the main herd. The house accommodated a farm worker. In the 1950s the land near the cottage was sold for building.

Moat House Farm

Jonathon Renton, aged 75, was the farmer at Moat House Farm in 1841. By 1851 George Clough was working on the farm with his widowed Aunt, Mary Renton, and subsequently took over the farm. He farmed there until the 1880s, with help from his nephew, George Kay. Tom Burnett took over the farm in the 1880s but by 1915 the farm was no longer a separate holding. The land was amalgamated with Manor Farm. The house was sold as a separate dwelling in 1950 and the farm buildings are now the Doctor's surgery.

Darley House Farm

In 1841 Henry Bullock, a native of East Keswick, farmed the 54-acre farm. It was situated at Darley House on Main Street. In 1861 his son Henry was working on the farm with his 85-year-old father. When Henry died in the 1880s the farm was split up and most of the land went to larger farms. The farmhouse had 6 ½ acres of land leading down to East Keswick Beck, described as 'poor grass and very wet and covered with weeds'. In 1893 the tenant, Mawson Taylor, was a teacher of music and sub-postmaster. It is probable that the fields were sublet.

Pasture House Farm

This farm on Moor Lane was a 53-acre holding in 1841, farmed by Joseph Clough, a native of East Keswick. His son, William, took over the farm until his death in the 1880s. At this time over 20 acres were transferred to neighbouring farms. Dan Barber, brother of Thomas at Ivy Grange, farmed here in the early twentieth century. After 1927, with further loss of land, to this time to Keswick Moor Farm, the farmhouse and remaining land was taken over by Manor Farm.

In 1886 there was a five-acre smallholding between North View and the Church, farmed by the Child family, who were described as cottagers. In 1927 the holding was 11 acres but sometime after this date it was absorbed into Field House Farm. Luptons bought it in 1950, using it as a quarantine unit for non-tuberculin tested cattle. In the 1960s a new housing estate on Church Drive and St Mary's Garth was built on the land. Council houses were built on land known as Child's Garth. A new unit of flats was built down Church Drive in 1972.

Nurseries and Market Gardens

Avenue Nursery

In 1871 James Allison of Avenue Nursery, on Harewood Avenue, was the only market gardener in East Keswick. On the purchase of The Nurseries by Harewood in 1878, James Firth of Farnley, 'a sober careful man', took over the tenancy. In 1917 the Firth family had a stall in Leeds Covered Market. The Firths were still in business in the 1940s.

Valley Nurseries

This was started by four brothers, Walter, James, Alfred and William Ridsdale from Bilbrough in the 1880s. They advertised as high-class florists in 1909. In 1915 they were renting land and houses but later Walter Ridsdale purchased Valley Nurseries on Moor Lane.

As a boy in the 1930s his grandson Mr Stanley Ridsdale preferred helping at Dalbys, at hay time, harvest and other busy periods, to working in the family business - ' a bit of a tedious job when you're a young kid having to go round weeding, especially in wintertime when it was cold.'

They sent a lot of cut flowers to Manchester and supplied local shops with bouquets and wreaths. He can remember his aunt going to Leeds market every day and his father delivering produce by pony and trap two or three times a week depending on the season. Stanley had to leave Tadcaster Grammar School at fifteen to work on the nursery. In the winter months he helped at threshing days on the local farms when nursery work was slack. 'It was a good job, better paid than the garden'. Before farmers in East Keswick got their own machines they used contractors - Bob Kay from Spofforth and Ted Rhodes from Wike. In 1943 Mr Ridsdale joined the Navy, spending two years on foreign commission in the Far East. The Nursery had to stop growing flowers in the war and produce vegetables instead.

The nursery continued until the 1970s and the land was then sold for housing.

Rose Nurseries

John Longfellow rented the nurseries from the Midgley family in the 1890s, eventually buying it in 1912. It passed to his nephew, Wilfred Stead, in 1929. It was sold to Ben Cooke in 1948. 'He wasn't very enthusiastic at gardening. He cleared off and went to Africa.' He sold it in 1951 to Mr and Mrs Hardisty, when it changed from a retail to a wholesale business. In 1965 50,000 pot plants were grown in the greenhouses. By 1971 the nurseries were greatly reduced in size and building had begun on a group of approximately thirty houses known as Rosecroft.

Whitegates

On Whitegate there was a 6-acre poultry farm and market garden, run by Mrs Duthoit for several years from 1935.

Ashfield Nurseries

Records of 1915 describe a nursery on the site of a former farm in Whitegate owned by Mr Sawer. He had left by the late 1940s and sold the land to Mr Cowling 'a wholesale fruit and veg chap in Leeds Market', who used it as a private residence only. The land has since been developed for building.

Moorside Poultry Farm

This was 8½ acres in 1943 and farmed by William and Gerald Wright. It is probable that it had been a market garden in the late nineteenth century as Charles Wright was described as a market gardener in 1893.

Moor Gardens

EJ Allison bought this as the sitting tenant from the Midgleys in 1907. Mrs Brierley remembers Ned Allison 'used to feed up pigs for fattening, which most people in the village did; they'd have a pig which would see them through the winter.'

Moor Gardens

There were several other properties with commercial greenhouses in the village in 1915, for example, a small market garden off School Lane, rented by Mr Bassitt. Tom Bowman had a market garden on an acre of land, where 'Danetree' is now situated.

By 1965 there were three nurseries in the village - Valley Nurseries, Rose Nurseries and Mr Mawson's Nursery on Moor Lane, which sold directly to the public. It closed in 1968. In 1972 'The Pines' nursery on Moor Lane was opened and a house built on the site. In 1965 Mr Matthews reared 7,500 hens at Cleavesty Lane Poultry Farm but by 1973 it had become a private residence and riding school. Lan-Dev Nurseries on Harewood Road started up in 1977.

East Keswick Farms in the World Wars

Both World Wars resulted in a need to increase food production. In January 1918 the West Riding Agricultural Executive Committee required eight farmers in East Keswick to plough specified acreages of permanent grassland to cultivate as arable and to grow wheat, oats and potatoes. The records are silent about the impact on the village farming community of so much loss of life in the First World War.

At the outbreak of the Second World War, Committees were again set up with the purpose of increasing food production with the power to direct types of cultivation, inspect property, dispossess the farmer and take over the tenancy and mobilise workers

Farm/Smallholding	Cows and Heifers in Milk	Total Cattle	Sheep	Pigs	Poultry
Manor Farm	30	72	50	0	0
Keswick Moor Farm	0	48	142	0	150
Field House Farm	43	91	107	6	12
Vicarage Farm	6	22	44	1	359
Old Hall Farm	10	47	0	4	71
Moor End Farm	2	19	0	12	126
North View	5	6	0	3	24
Stocks Hill	4	8	0	0	0
Argyle Farm	2	8	0	3	40
South View	-	12	0	5	5

to work on the farms. The second National Farm Survey 1941-43 had the long-term purpose of providing information for post war agricultural planning. In addition to the usual annual June 4th returns in which the farmers provided detailed information on crop acreages and livestock numbers, inspectors visited all agricultural holdings of five acres and over, assessing in detail the condition and management of the farm. The management of a farm was Classified as A (well managed), B (fairly managed) or C (badly managed). Three of the nine farms in East Keswick received an A rating. The reasons given for B and C ratings were variously attributed to old age, bad health, lack of farming knowledge, lack of capital and insufficient time spent on the holding.

The extent of livestock production in the village in 1941 can be gauged from the table above.

This chapter illustrates how, in the last fifty years, all the smallholdings, nurseries and market gardens within the village have disappeared to become private residences and housing estates.

The *East Keswick W.I. Farming Year Book* of 1989 noted the feeling of uncertainty among farmers concerning government and European agricultural policies and their possible effects on the medium and small stock and mixed farms. In the new millennium it seems the doubt extends to all of farming in Britain… Only time will tell.

A note on sources

Most of the earlier information about farming came from the Harewood Archives, such as manorial records, rentals, accounts, tenancy agreements, surveys, maps, estate correspondence. 'Scrapbooks' of local records belonging to the Teal family in the eighteenth and early nineteenth centuries, also deposited at Sheepscar, provided additional information. Further information relating to East Keswick was gathered from the census returns 1841-91, parliamentary papers, including the agricultural returns (MAF 68) in the Public Record Office, local newspapers and trade directories.

Present and former villagers kindly provided information that added meat to the bones of the major twentieth century archive sources - namely the Field Books (IR 58) forming part of the Valuation records in the Public Record Office, resulting from The Finance (1909-1910) Act, and the National Farm Surveys 1940-1943. The Women's Institute surveys of the village in 1965 and 1977 and of the farms in 1989 were useful sources of information.

Mrs F Brierley née Dalby,
Mrs A Dawson née Blackburn,
Mr Derek Illingworth
Mr D Lupton
Mr Stanley Ridsdale

7

Religion

East Keswick was part of the Parish of Harewood along with a collection of surrounding villages. All these villages until the nineteenth century had their focus of Anglican worship in Harewood. Gradually the outlying areas have become separated from Harewood and finally the church in Harewood was closed in the 1970s. The presence of rich families would be a reason why churches were built in communities in early times and, more recently, the presence of larger populations would also lead to churches being built. The fact that the parish was so large and contained quite separate communities may be taken as an indication that none of them contained many people or much wealth. Until the death of Lady Elizabeth Hastings there exists no suggestion that East Keswick should possess its own Anglican church. Lady Elizabeth Hastings was an extremely wealthy and pious lady who owned the tithes of the village and proposed bequeathing the tithes to support a church. Perhaps this may suggest that previously no person of wealth and piety had been connected with the village. Additionally the increasing influence of nonconformists after the Civil War (and increasing population) may have influenced Lady Hastings to suggest the establishment of a separate church for East Keswick though this was rejected by the inhabitants. Thus the earliest physical signs of religion in East Keswick are concerned with Quakerism and later on Methodism.

The Quakers of East Keswick

The first evidence of Quakers in East Keswick is in 1665 when Sarah Marshall, a widow, was imprisoned presumably for non-payment of tithes. It is interesting that the influence of the Quakers should have spread to East Keswick so quickly when George Fox only began his ministry in the 1650s.

The next evidence is the Quaker burial ground which was situated in the area around Clitheroe Cottage. It was a walled plot and occupied an area of about 60 square yards. The reasons for having a specifically 'Quaker' burial ground were that in the late seventeenth century, persons not baptised were not eligible to be buried in consecrated ground, were sometimes excommunicated, were refused burial by the local Parish priest or were themselves unwilling to be buried in traditionally consecrated ground. In the immediate vicinity there were Quaker burial grounds at Tadcaster, York, Leeds, Pontefract and Sherburn.

The land on which the burial ground was sited was owned by the Wright family of Lofthouse Farm. The first burial recorded was that of Peter Wright in 1689 and the last recorded was Hannah Daniel in 1794. The plan of the burial ground shows twenty interments but, according to Thistlethwaite, the burial records suggest thirty-four. In all there are four family names associated with the graveyard - Wright, Stead, Kilby and Daniel. There is a tantalising reference to a William Kilby in the record of a 'Lay Subsidy' in 1725 which says 'this lay is supposed to have been drawn out by one William Kilby who was a schoolmaster, a blanket weaver by trade and a Quaker - and at that time did the Town's business'. It is tempting to see this William Kilby as the son of the above family who is recorded as born in East Keswick in 1693 and died in Castleford in 1776.

The Quakers of East Keswick and surrounding area had their meetings at Clifford until 1790. At that time so few were attending the Clifford Meeting House that it was closed and the remaining members were transferred to other houses. Joseph Wright of Lofthouse was transferred to Brighouse!

The land for a graveyard was given by Peter Wright. There are indentures of 1711, 1731 and 1768 conveying the land from one set of trustees to another. In 1796 the Harewood Estate survey of the Township of East Keswick records the graveyard as being owned by the trustees of the Methodist Church. This may be so but in 1851 the minutes of the Monthly Friends' Meeting in York records the acceptance by the Earl of Harewood of the burial ground on condition that it be not dug or built on. The reason for the sale was that no burials had been carried out in the last half century.

In 1890 the care of the burial ground was entrusted to a Miss Laurence who was the tenant of the adjacent cottage. In 1951 the burial ground was sold to Mrs Wood then the owner of the adjacent cottage.

Methodism in East Keswick

There are records of house prayer meetings being held in East Keswick from 1777. Evidence of local hostility to the Methodists is shown in the breaking of the windows of a house in Bardsey whilst a meeting was being held.

Permission was obtained from the Archbishop in York for a chapel to be built in East Keswick. In 1791 land was bought in School Lane for five shillings on which to build the chapel. As a sideline on the state of education in the village, seven of the trustees made their mark rather than signing, whereas in 1818 when new trustees were appointed, all of them signed.

The new chapel was opened on Christmas Day 1792 by the Rev Joseph Entwistle who had known John Wesley and was later to become one of the first presidents of the

Methodist Chapel, Main Street

Joseph Laurence 1819 - 1886

Methodist Conference. The date 1792 is still visible on the gable end facing Main Street.

Methodism must have flourished in the village because by the middle of the next century land was being purchased (1844) for a new Wesleyan Chapel and a Primitive Methodist Chapel (1847). The latter at the top of Whitegate in the house now named 'Hillside' has a plaque outside with the date 1847. Whether this was the date the building began to be used or when the foundation stone was laid is unclear. The register of baptisms begins in December 1849 and continues until 1875 although only seventeen names are listed. Apparently the registers may not be entirely accurate as they were compiled on a circuit basis and not by each individual chapel. It is said that the chapel was converted into a private house in 1900.

Returning to the Wesleyan Chapel, although land was purchased in 1844, the new chapel was not built until 1891 by which time it was not simply a matter of replacing the old Chapel in School Lane.

Joseph Laurence was born in 1819, the fifth of ten children. George Laurence, his father, was born in Spofforth in 1788 and his occupation is given as farmer/schoolteacher. His eldest child, Mary, was born in Alwoodley in 1814 and the second child, William, was born in East Keswick in 1815. In East Keswick he founded or took over a boarding school which is recorded in the 1841 census as having 43 pupils, both boys and girls. Six of his ten children are recorded as being teachers.

Joseph is not recorded in the 1841 census for East Keswick and presumably was working or training as a teacher elsewhere. By 1851 he had returned to East Keswick and was teaching at his father's school which he later took over. He then began the work for which he is famous. He converted the school into a preparatory theological college for Methodist Ministers intending to serve as missionaries. When he died in 1886 it is said that more than sixty had gone to Newfoundland and others to Australia, New Zealand, India and Africa. Many of these students' education had been financially assisted by Laurence who had even paid for their outfits. Beginning in 1875, the Newfoundland Methodist Conference annual minutes 'express its great obligation to Joseph Laurence, Esq. of East Keswick, Yorkshire, England, for the many practical proofs he has afforded of his interest in the spiritual prosperity of this Colony, and especially for his painstaking exertion in procuring and forwarding so many candidates for our Ministry.' These votes of thanks continued yearly until 1887, when the Conference sent its sympathy to Laurence's family after learning of his death: 'Our church in this colony owes a debt of gratitude to Mr Lawrence [sic] which can never be discharged.'

After his death many letters of appreciation were sent from all over the world by former students. There was also a presentation book of photographs compiled in Newfoundland and sent *in memoriam*. This book was returned to Newfoundland, in 1964 to the then president of Newfoundland, JR Smallwood, who bequeathed it to the Centre for Newfoundland Studies Archives, Memorial University of Newfoundland, in 1992.

It is said that the memorial chapel opened on Easter Monday 1891 was paid for by donations from his past students. Whether this be the case or not, the chapel opened free of debt and was named 'Joseph Laurence Memorial Chapel'. In 1981 the name was changed to 'East Keswick Methodist Church'. In the light of the above, one regrets the omission of the illustrious name 'Laurence' from the church's name.

Church of St Mary Magdalene

Until 1856 there was no Anglican place of worship in East Keswick and the villagers would have travelled to Harewood for services, as indeed they must have done since the area was settled. When Lady Elizabeth Hastings died in 1739, she bequeathed the tithes of East Keswick to the villagers on condition that they built a chapel. Failing this the money would pass to the parish of Harewood. Apparently there was no agreement from the villagers forthcoming and the gift was forfeited - 'In the judgement of the authors of *East Keswick Remembered*, this was the greatest misfortune that ever befell East Keswick'. It is not at all clear what was meant by this remark unless it is simply an expression of regret that there was no Church of England place of worship in East Keswick for a further hundred years. As there are no records surviving which give details of the reasons for the decision the villagers took, one can only mention the background to the case. In 1676 the population of East Keswick is given elsewhere as between 150 and 180. Allowing that it was growing, it is unlikely to have been in excess of 250 by 1739. There were a number of Quaker families in the village. A Methodist chapel was built in the village only fifty years later. The ownership of the Harewood estate, by coincidence, changed hands in 1739, the very year that Lady Elizabeth Hastings died.

The church was finally built in 1856 by public subscription but by then the population had grown to 450, there were no Quakers in the village and the Harewood Estate owners were well settled. The Earl of Harewood contributed to the costs as well as donating the land. The church was designed by the Bradford architects Mallinson and Healey in an unornamented Gothic style. A Curate in Charge was appointed under the Vicar of Harewood.

Banns could not be read nor marriages solemnized until a licence was granted in 1896.

Refurbishment and improvements of various kinds have been undertaken but the structure remains virtually unaltered since its construction. Beginning with altar rails in 1957 a series of purchases of oak furniture from 'Mouseman' Thompson of Kilburn have been made.

In 1953, due to a shortage of clergy, East Keswick was without a Curate and the Vicar of Harewood took over the running of both churches and East Keswick vicarage was sold. On the death of Canon Griffith in 1974, East Keswick was taken out of the Parish of Harewood and transferred to Bardsey Parish, Harewood church was closed and Harewood transferred to the Parish of Collingham.

St Mary Magdalene

Sources

A Bygone Quaker Meeting by WP Thistlethwiate
The Church of St Mary Magdalene, East Keswick (pamphlet)
The East Keswick Methodist Centenary Booklet (1991)
East Keswick Remembered

8

East Keswick schools and schooldays - education for all: 1815-1914

Schooling in East Keswick has a long history. From its beginnings in the early nineteenth century it developed on two levels, on one hand public elementary education, destined for the labouring classes of the area, and on the other private schools for the sons and daughters of the emergent middle classes of Victorian England. The first of these was incorporated into the state system of primary education we are familiar with today, the second flourished before being overtaken by the forces of social change. But different though they were in their purpose and form, these two types of educational provision shared important features: each had its origins in wholly local initiatives and each was connected in some way with organised religion. This chapter attempts to chart these parallel paths and identify how each in its way enriched the life of the community in which it was located.

Local trends in education cannot be considered in isolation, since they combine to form part of a larger national picture. Any examination of schooling in East Keswick, therefore, must take some account of the political and social events which helped to form it and which ultimately brought about its demise, leaving the village without its school and, arguably, diminishing the quality of life for the villagers it was set up to serve.

Public elementary education in East Keswick: the early years

Previous researchers into the history of public education in East Keswick have found hard information on the origins of the village school very elusive. However it does seem likely that it developed from a Sunday school set up in about 1814 by Rev Richard Hale, who was Vicar of Harewood and Domestic Chaplain to the Earl. In the absence of any national education system at this time it was through Sunday schools that some notions of literacy were first dispensed to England's untutored masses.

Since the middle of the eighteenth century, these schools, set up as voluntary initiatives on the part of the Church of England and the Nonconformists, had been spreading rapidly through the country in response to a new national belief that illiteracy was a moral problem. Though dominated inevitably by Religious Instruction, the schools' curricula included reading, so bringing new skills to a neglected and growing sector of the population, the urban and rural poor. One historian has described the Sunday school movement as a phenomenon unparalleled in the history of education, laying as it did the foundations of life-long learning in many of its pupils.

The governing classes favoured Sunday schools as much as a means of social control as an educational benefit, though they needed constant reassurance that the poor were not being educated beyond the requirements of the place they were to occupy in society. It was not uncommon, when the establishment of a Sunday school was proposed and sponsorship sought from local gentry, for some statement to be made about the prospective school's purpose. The following is fairly typical: 'The children are to be taught to read and to be instructed in the plain duties of the Christian religion with a particular view to their good and industrious behaviour in their future character of Labourers and Servants.' The inculcation of habits of deference and obedience was therefore an integral part of the Sunday schools' purpose from the outset.

Both the English aristocracy and the Church were mindful of the social turmoil that had so recently been unleashed in France by the Revolution of 1789, when organised religion had become outlawed, the church's property confiscated and the flower of French nobility trundled unceremoniously to the guillotine. At home, the worrying outbreaks of civil disorder that had punctuated the later years of the reign of George III seemed to suggest that England might be experiencing the birth of its own revolutionary tradition. It was small wonder, then, that the government of the day supported any means by which the common people might be conditioned to habits of order and respect for authority. For six days a week the children of the poor presented few problems, since they tended to be occupied in various kinds of manual labour. But on their day off it was not infrequent for them to indulge in riotous behaviour. In the words of one contemporary observer, 'farmers and other inhabitants of the towns and villages receive more injury to their property in the Sabbath than in all the week besides; this in a great measure proceeds from the lawless state of the younger class who are allowed to run wild on that day free from every restraint'.

There is no particular evidence to suggest that the youth of East Keswick ran riot in this way or that the establishment of the Sunday school was anything other than one of the many notable philanthropic gestures by the Earl of Harewood. However it would be unreasonable to suppose that the village children in the early Eighteen Hundreds were very different from their counterparts elsewhere in the country and it would be surprising also if the local clergy and the Earl were unaware of the vigorous national debate which was taking place on the education of the poor. East Keswick Sunday school, therefore, would have been typical of similar institutions which proliferated during the later eighteenth and early nineteenth centuries. Moreover we know from contemporary sources that in East Keswick every poor person's child was afforded the opportunity of learning to read at the Sunday school (though no mention is made of how many took this opportunity or learnt to write) and that all children aged twelve and over in the village could repeat the catechism.

Despite their remarkable success, it soon became obvious that Sunday schools alone were insufficient to meet the challenge of the task of educating the lower classes. Little by little, and again on the initiative of philanthropic donors and religious reformers, a system of day schools emerged which offered a broader and more diverse curriculum than was possible in the Sunday schools. Chief providers of day schools at this time were the Church of England's National Society, founded in 1811, and the British and Foreign School Society which had its origins in the work of the Quaker Joseph Lancaster.

As early as 1813 some 230 National schools were in existence, including one at Harewood, operating the monitorial system promoted by the Society's founder, Rev Andrew Bell. Under this system, all pupils in a school were taught together by one teacher assisted by older pupils, the so-called monitors. Though hardly ideal in terms of providing quality education, the system had the great merit for its proponents of being exceedingly cheap to operate.

In East Keswick the extension of educational provision from a Sunday to a day school probably took place shortly after the Hale initiative, when Church-sponsored elementary schools were experiencing something of a boom time nationally. Though independent of the National Society at this time, the village school had close links with the church and was to retain its voluntary status throughout its history.

It seems likely that the new day school that was planned for the village replaced an earlier school, since records from the mid-eighteenth century refer to a School House owned by a Mr James Bradley and located in West Field. The Bradleys appear to have been a family of some academic distinction, for the grave of James Bradley (probably the son of the owner of School House) mentions the 'Eminence he attained in mathematical and other useful branches of Science' and records that 'in genius and worth he was excelled by few'. In a Latin plaque on the same tomb, another Bradley, Jacob, is remembered as a loyal friend and distinguished doctor.

If the Bradley establishment was indeed a school, it must have been a small affair, probably dispensing a traditional classical education to a select group of boys from the more prosperous families in the area. The new school, however, was designed for a much more diverse population. It appears to have been a simple one-storey building with a single classroom measuring 30 feet by 12. This would lend itself exactly to the type of monitorial teaching favoured by the National Society. Using the current accepted norm of about six square feet per pupil, the maximum number of pupils for which the school was designed would have been in the order of 60. In fact, according to Rev Hale's own calculations there were 89 children in the village who in 1815 were 'capable of receiving instruction', 62 of whom attended the Sunday school and 20 the day school. 20 children were apparently not in receipt of any public instruction at all. Those who did attend would, of course, have spanned the elementary school age range of five to twelve and would have all been taught together in the single schoolroom.

A team of builders and craftsmen was assembled for the construction of the school under the direction of the Harewood stonemason John Muschamp, whose grandfather had built Harewood House. But, although there remains little doubt that the school was actually constructed, its exact location remains a tantalising mystery. Various sites have been suggested, including the area of Burns Farm and a location south of Keswick Beck in the vicinity of Hemingways' pig farm. However, the 1850 Ordnance Survey map of Harewood Parish shows a 'parochial school' close to the present day School Lane, a central location which would have obvious advantages of accessibility for village children and seems the most sensible position for a school. If this was so, the problem of locations is only half solved, for, according to the Education Returns supplied to Parliament in 1833, there were actually two day schools in the village: the one described above and a second, which had opened in the previous year and was attended by 14 girls, all educated at the expense of their parents. The nature and site of this second school remain a mystery, though it seems likely that since it was entirely fee-paying it was set up to cater for a rather higher stratum of village society than the church school. It may be that this school was or became the Wesleyan school which was reported to exist in the village in the Post Office directories of 1857 and 1861, a possibility strengthened by the fact that the school was single-sex. Funding for the village school, which in 1833 had 15 boys and five girls on roll, came from two sources, an annual allowance of 13 guineas from the Earl, which provided free education for six pupils, and fees charged to parents of the remaining 14 children. The master's responsibilities, in addition to teaching the day pupils, also included superintendence of the Sunday school, where as many as 56 children now received instruction.

By 1851, the number of children at the school was about 50 out of a total village population of about 450, each paying a penny a week to follow a basic curriculum with a heavy religious education component. The church continued to play a significant if not dominant part in influencing events at the school, and pupils were subject to regular inspections from Diocesan officers. But by this time, reports of alarming shortcomings in Bell's monitorial system were becoming widespread. It was alleged that in some schools nothing but reading and selected portions of the prayer book were being taught and where writing was prohibited by the clergyman in charge because 'the boys would merely learn to scribble on the walls and palings'. Moreover, such was the demand for agricultural labour in rural areas such as East Keswick that fewer than 10% of pupils stayed beyond the age of ten. They were employed instead to 'drive teams, tend the cows and watch the birds'. As will be seen later, this diversion of children away from education into farm work was to remain an acute problem in East Keswick until well into the next century.

It was at about this time that the National Society was compelled to accept proposals for the reform of its schools. Local vicars, who had had complete control of the elementary curriculum hitherto, were to remain in charge of religious education only, the rest of the curriculum being handed over to the care of a local committee. The church predictably saw this measure as an erosion of its influence in the vital area of education but was forced to comply under the threat of compelling legislation.

We can gain some idea of the state of public education in the East Keswick area in the latter half of the nineteenth century from the evidence presented to a Royal Commission in 1867 by CR Moorsom, agent to Lord Harewood, and by churchmen and farmers representing the villages in Harewood parish. Though labour was not abundant in this area owing to the proximity of manufacturing towns, which drew off young men at a rate of wages higher than was paid for agricultural work, it was said to be rare for women and children to be employed in field work. No boys under 14, according to the farmers, 'went to the field', but they did admit that attendance at schools throughout the district was patchy. Parents were described as being very indifferent about the education and schooling of their children, though the farmers stated that most of the young and middle-aged population of the district could read and write. Increased government support would also help in their view, since although there was no shortage of schools in the area, these were often were very poor and 'had bad masters'.

It is difficult to tell how far the need to pay fees was a disincentive for parents to send their children to school. We know that school fees in Wetherby in the 1860s ranged from 1d to 4d a week for the labouring classes, that the ordinary rate of wages for an agricultural worker was 14 shillings a week in the Harewood area and that the average rent of a two-up two-down cottage was one shilling a week. So, as a proportion of income, school fees were not high in themselves but would be more so in real terms if children spent their time in school rather than in the fields, where they might expect to earn sixpence a day for 'bird tenting' and a shilling for pea-picking. In these circumstances it would be very unusual if needy parents consistently ignored the earning potential of their children, and it is highly likely that school attendance was seasonal: higher in winter months and much lower at times of planting and harvest. Soon, however, the choice of whether to send their children to school or not was to be removed from parents: the age of compulsory elementary education was about to dawn.

At national level, the progress of educational thinking during the latter half of the nineteenth century made state-funded education an inevitability. The provision made by religious agencies like the National Society and its Nonconformist counterparts was localised, leaving great areas of the country, particularly the industrial conurbations, without any educational provision whatever. Only state intervention could make up this shortfall and in 1870 the Forster Education Act introduced a requirement for the establishment of School Boards to provide rate-funded schools in areas where elementary education was deemed unsatisfactory or insufficient. This landmark event had the effect of making elementary education compulsory and reshaping it as a public service for the first time in this country.

The parliamentary debate which led up to Forster's Act and the prospect of imminent educational reform were undoubtedly influential in the formulation of plans for a new school to replace the now antiquated building designed by Muschamp, for it is certain that all-age teaching in a single room would prove unacceptable to inspectors from the Education Department in the post-Forster era. A new school was needed and was duly built, incorporating living accommodation for the head teacher and financed once again by the Earl of Harewood. The new school was situated in Moor Lane, almost opposite the then recently constructed church. Almost immediately, it began to benefit from parliamentary grants. Attendance levels between the school's opening in about 1870 and the end of the century grew from 38 to about 50, an increase which was reflected in a rise in its grant from £12.10.8d in 1872 to £39.19.0d in 1895. From the evidence of census returns and contemporary press references it seems also that the new school became affiliated to the National Society at about this time. In 1881 and 1891 the mistress of the school, Elizabeth Moore, is described as 'National school teacher'. If this information is correct, financial support for the school would have been forthcoming from the Society to supplement government grants and parental payments. The school would have faced the advent of the new century on a sound financial footing.

Colleges, Academies and Seminaries: private education in East Keswick 1830-1900

Among the papers relating to the building of the public elementary school in 1815 are the names of various craftsmen employed by the Harewood Estate to carry out the work. Also mentioned is a Mr Lawrence, who is listed as 'schoolmaster'. We must assume that this is the George Lawrence (later to be spelt Laurence) mentioned in the 1822 *Baines Directory of Yorkshire*. It seems that shortly afterwards George made a move from the public to the private sector of education, since by the 1830s we know that he had established his own boarding school in Clitheroe House, School Lane.

The school, which came to be known variously as Keswick School (1867), East Keswick Commercial and Collegiate School (1873) and East Keswick Collegiate School (1875) prospered during these years, receiving up to 55 boys aged between nine and 17. It may be that this school had some connection with the Wesleyan school referred to in contemporary directories, although no mention is made of any religious affiliation in the various advertisements which appeared in Yorkshire newspapers. It is only when George Laurence's son Joseph, who was a convert to Methodism, took over the school that its orientation changed to assume a more obviously religious dimension.

For most of its life, the school was set up to deliver a broadly-based academic curriculum to the sons of middle class parents. It is evident from census records that pupils were recruited from a wide area, a large proportion coming from the industrial towns and cities of the Pennines. A number also came from the villages surrounding East Keswick, and it may be that some further pupils were day boys from East Keswick itself. The school offered teaching by certificated teachers in English, French, German, Music,

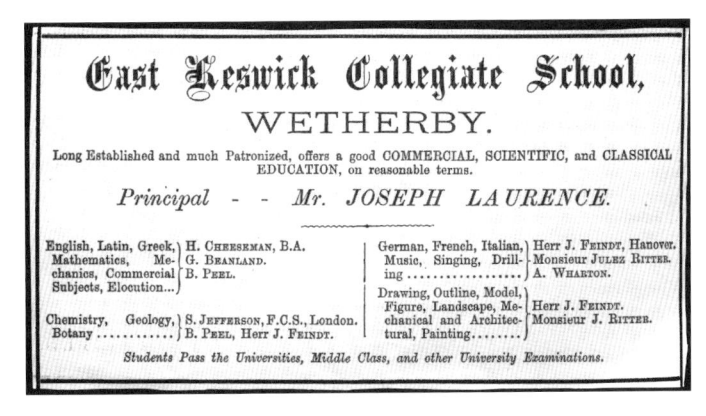

Advertisement, White's Clothing District Directory, 1875

Pages from a pupil's copy book, George Laurence's Academy, 1834. (Photos courtesy of Ron Sudderdean)

Singing, Drawing and the Physical Sciences and, as the school expanded, there was provision also for Greek, Latin, Mechanics, Geology, and a range of other subjects, including 'Outline, Model, Landscape, Mechanical and Architectural Drawing'. Perhaps the most unexpected subject to appear on the curriculum of this boys' school was elocution. At its most prosperous period, when Joseph became principal after his father's death, the Laurence school employed nine masters, including native French and German teachers of modern languages. Fees were advertised, unsurprisingly, as 'reasonable' and students were said to pass 'the Universities, Middle Class and other University Examinations'. To provide more accommodation as the number of boarders grew, an extra building had been erected in about 1850 on a vacant piece of land abutting School House at the end of School Lane. It was here that classes were held until the school's demise at the turn of the century. After remaining unoccupied for some years, the building, which remained the property of the Harewood estate, eventually became the home of the village elementary school.

The orientation of Joseph Laurence's work changed at some point after he took over his father's school to focus on, or at least encompass, the training of young men for the Methodist ministry and for missionary work overseas. In a commemorative volume compiled in appreciation of Laurence following his death in 1886, his work both for the locality of East Keswick and abroad is highly praised. In what came to be known as Keswick Preparatory College, Laurence taught free of charge a number of local young men some of whom took up ministries in Newfoundland. In 1875 the Methodist Conference of that country expressed its 'great obligation to Joseph Laurence ... for the many practical proofs he has afforded of his interest in the spiritual prosperity of this Colony, and especially for his painstaking exertion in procuring and forwarding to this country so many candidates for our Ministry.' These votes of thanks continued annually until 1887, when the Conference sent its sympathy to the Laurence family after learning of Joseph's death. Testimonies to Joseph's work include one from a former pupil, who described his teacher as 'perhaps the most painstaking, conscientious and affable man I have ever known.' After Joseph's death, the College was taken over by a Rev HB Kendall, but it seems that without its founder's inspiration and commitment it continued in existence only a short time longer. Laurence's memory was perpetuated when the village's Methodist Church, built at a cost of £1645 and opened in 1891, was given its formal title, 'The Laurence Memorial Wesleyan Methodist Chapel and Sunday School'. Though this title was discontinued in 1981, a commemorative plaque in the church serves as a reminder of Laurence's life and work.

The Laurence family's involvement in education was complemented on the female side by Joseph's sisters, Mary and Louisa, who are described in census returns as governesses. Louisa, like Joseph, became a member of the College of Preceptors before the age of 20, so gaining a teaching qualification at a time when lack of certification amongst practising teachers in both the private and public sectors was widespread. By 1851 the sisters had their own private girls' school, located initially in School Lane and, after their father's death and the expansion of the boys' boarding school, at The Mount on Cleavesty Lane, which had been built in about 1850 and became the Laurence family home.

The sisters were, according to their press advertisements, assisted by 'experienced governesses' and, in keeping with the current expectations of the parents of 'young ladies', the curriculum they offered had a distinctly female orientation. Instruction included English, French, Elementary Drawing, Singing, Music and Dancing. The latter two subjects were considered 'extras' and attracted additional fees, as did tuition in the somewhat arcane skill of modelling wax flowers. Annual fees were graduated according to pupils' ages, ranging from 24 guineas for girls in the eight to ten age group to 28 guineas for those between the ages of 12 and 14. The number of pupils enrolled at the

The Laurence Ladies' Seminary at the Mount around 1890

school never equalled those of at the boys' College, averaging between 14 and 24 in the years 1851-1871, but, like their male counterparts, girls came mostly from the industrial towns of the West Riding.

The Misses Laurence's Ladies' Seminary, as the school was called, and their brother's College were typical of the small private institutions of this kind which enjoyed considerable patronage during the latter half of the nineteenth century. Advertisements for such schools for both girls and boys abound at this period and testify that it was quite usual for villages outside the major conurbations to have their private academy or college. Nearby Shadwell, for example, boasted its Misses Snowden's school, Aberford its Misses Simpson's, while Boston Spa and Bramham each had its College, Thorp Arch its Grange School and Spofforth its Academy.

We know from contemporary press reports that the Laurences held annual concerts at Christmas time, using them on occasions as an opportunity for charity appeals. Joseph's entertainment of Christmas 1870, for example, raised funds for 'the homeless and starving people whose homes have been burnt in the war between France and Germany', Joseph himself making 'a heart-rending appeal from France'. Members of the Laurence family and their staff made various contributions to the entertainments. Joseph's daughters Helen and Mary Louisa performed songs and Mr Beanland, a teacher and clearly an annual favourite, gave 'humorous readings' which 'caused much mirth and laughter'. Much of the success of the concerts appears to have been due to the expertise of the music master, possibly the Hanover-born Herr Feindt, who taught German and French at the Academy. *The Northern Reporter* was effusive in its praise of his work:

> 'We cannot speak too highly of the abilities of Mr Laurence's music master and we feel certain that few villages can give such an entertainment as that given here previous to the Christmas vacation.'

Similar entertainments (referred to as soirées) were held at the girls' Seminary, and it may be that they, like those at the College, were thrown open to villagers, though it is evident that the occasion served also as a prize evening. The soirées were held in The Mount's 'spacious schoolroom' which was 'artistically decorated for the occasion with mottoes, devices, evergreens and flowers'. After songs performed by various young ladies, certificates for good character and proficiency in studies were distributed, after which those present enjoyed 'a bountiful repast'.

By 1908 the Laurence sisters had retired to Clitheroe House in School Lane. The Methodist Minute Book and Accounts for this period records that contributions towards the construction of the church were made both by the their own former pupils and by Joseph's former students in Newfoundland and Nova Scotia. Joseph's daughter, Mary Louisa, shared responsibility for the church choir after the 1891 opening but thereafter no mention is made of any Laurence association with the church. The long chapter of the family's educational work in the village had finally come to its close.

LADIES' SEMINARY,
THE MOUNT,
EAST KESWICK, NEAR WETHERBY.

CONDUCTED BY MISS LAURENCE,
Assisted by Experienced Governesses.

Terms:

Board, and Instruction in English, French, and Elementary Drawing:

For Pupils from Eight to Ten	24 Guineas per Annum.
„ from Ten to Twelve	26 „ „
„ from Twelve to Fourteen	28 „ „
Music, and the use of the Piano	4 „ „
The Modelling of Wax Flowers	1 „ „
Washing, Calisthenics, &c.	4 „ „

Approved Masters attend to teach Singing, Music, French, and Dancing.

Advertisement, Bean's Directory, 1873

The Harewood Literary and Scientific Institution

The history of education in East Keswick is not complete without a mention of the Harewood Literary and Scientific Institution, which was established in March 1853. Institutes of this kind spread widely during the first half of the Nineteenth century, the first being founded in London in 1823. More commonly known in the industrial towns as Mechanics Institutes, their aim was to provide avenues for self-advancement amongst the working classes by offering library facilities, lectures and evening classes. The institutes were to a large extent dependent on the patronage of the middle class and local gentry, whose organisational know-how and financial support ensured their viability.

The Harewood Institution occupied a 'large commodious apartment' in the village, provided by the Earl and comfortably fitted out with benches and tables by its committee. Opening times were from six o'clock on weekdays and three on Saturdays. On Sundays it was closed, no doubt to avoid standing as an alternative attraction to church attendance. Newspapers and journals were taken daily (*The Times* and the *Sun*), weekly (*The Leeds Intelligencer, Punch, Illustrated News*) or monthly (*Art Journal, The Veterinarian, The Mechanics Magazine, The Family Herald,* etc) and further reading opportunities were offered by the library, which contained 700 volumes, about half of which were donated by the Countess. Typical of the lecture programmes provided was that of November 1855 to April 1856 (i.e. the low season for agricultural work). Twelve lectures were arranged, covering a wide variety of topics including photography, the solar system and meteoric stones, Shakespeare, popular superstitions and incidents of the war. Members were admitted free to lectures and allowed to bring a lady. Non-members paid sixpence.

Evening classes were held on three evenings a week, taught by Rev Miles Atkinson the Vicar of Harewood and Mr Jones, the village schoolmaster. Instruction included writing, dictation, English grammar, arithmetic and mensuration. Classes were 'tolerably well attended' and were 'productive of much good'.

The Harewood Institution was seen as a model of excellence, one of the two chosen by Inspector of Schools Rev F Watkins to describe in detail to the Committee of the Privy Council in his annual report on educational provision in Yorkshire. Such organisations, he enthused, 'form an important part of the educational machinery of the country, quite as much as our National schools do, and are rendering incalculable service to the community, not only in instructing and aiding our adult population, but in taking charge of our future men at the most critical stage in their life, viz. from boyhood to manhood.'

One of the novel and innovatory features of the Institution was the establishment of a branch library at Weeton, one of the seven satellite townships of Harewood. A box of books was sent to the village every fortnight, and members paid two shillings a quarter for access to them. The arrangement proved so successful that at the time of Rev Watkins' 1856 report consideration was being given to extending it to East Keswick. It seems certain that this development did take place and become a part of village life, attracting artisans and labourers. The location of the branch library is not known, but it seems certain that it survived and maybe even grew through the second half of the century. In 1887 David Daniel is described in directories as secretary of the East Keswick Mechanics' Institute, though no subsequent reference to him is made.

In its small way, then, East Keswick was part of national upsurge in opportunities for working class education. The Mechanics' Institute movement continued in various forms into the twentieth century and can be seen as a precursor to such institutions as the Workers' Educational Association, Access courses and the Open University.

The village school, 1870-1914

In the public sector, meanwhile, the church elementary school went about its work under successive masters and mistresses. The school in Moor Lane had been built to accommodate 90 pupils, though in 1893 average attendance amounted to only about 50 out of the 73 village children who were described in census returns as 'scholars'. The pupils ranged in age from four to 16, with the majority in the 5-12 age group. Their family backgrounds were diverse, with the greatest proportion, predictably, being the children of agricultural labourers. Farmers' children made up the second largest group, followed by others from a wide variety of occupational backgrounds including shepherds, platelayers, law stationers, cordwainers and liverymen.

Attendance levels, problematic during the whole history of the school, often threatened the viability of its operations as well as causing organisational and educational problems within its day-to-day running. By 1904, however, average daily attendance had risen to 61 and it had become clear that the present accommodation was imposing restrictions on the type of teaching that could be given. Though obviously an improvement on the single room arrangement of Muschamp's building, it is clear from contemporary records that in the Moor Lane premises opportunities for head teacher William Worthy (who had succeeded Mr Harrison as head in 1902) to separate the three divisions of pupils (Class I, Class II and Infants) into homogeneous age groups were still limited. The type of teaching available, therefore, could not be targeted at particular years as is

The village school at Moor Lane, 1901, with head teacher Mr Harrison.
(Photo courtesy of Joan Waide)

common (though not universal) practice in primary schools today.

The twentieth century was not far advanced before the need for more spacious accommodation became a matter of urgency. It was decided finally that the buildings in School Lane previously occupied by Joseph Laurence's College would meet current criteria for efficient schooling and preparations were put in train for the move to take place. One of His Majesty's Inspectors of Schools noted in 1910 that children would be shortly transferred to more convenient premises which might 'give opportunity for the introduction of Cottage Gardening and Manual Instruction for boys and Domestic Training for girls'. Meanwhile, in keeping with developments in educational technology of the day, his advice was that 'slates should be less used and their place taken by exercise books, which will more readily show pupils' daily progress'.

Throughout the early years of the century the pattern of daily life in the school was occasionally interrupted by village events. Whole-day holidays were given for Harewood Feast, parliamentary elections and the village 'turn out' to the seaside, and pupils enjoyed a half-holiday each Shrove Tuesday. Other, less happy, closures were ordered when the school was hit by epidemics of scarlet fever (two weeks in 1910), mumps (four weeks in 1912) and measles (two weeks in 1912). In addition, attendance levels continued to be seriously affected in the summer months by the need for pupils to help

> The annual prize giving took place on Wednesday October 26th at 3 pm. After prayers had been said by the Curate-in-charge, the prizes were presented by the Countess of Harewood, who has, for several years, generously provided them as an incentive to regular attendance. There were also present the Rev. M.G. and Mrs Lascelles, and Mrs Travis of Ripley. Twenty six of the scholars received books, and seven of these, who had never been absent from school during the past year were awarded medals in addition. During the afternoon a few songs were sung by the scholars, after which hearty cheers were given for their kind friends and teachers. Later on all sat down to an excellent tea, kindly given by the Vicar and Mrs Lascelles. In the evening the Curate-in-charge gave a lantern entertainment showing many very beautiful views, and then games, recreations, etc. were the absorbing interest until 9 o'clock, when all went home thoroughly pleased with a very happy day.

The Northern Reporter and Knaresborough and Wetherby Advertiser,
5 November 1904.

with haymaking and in the winter by inclement weather. When Lady Harewood made her usual visit to the school in 1911 for the annual distribution of prizes and medals, only 17 pupils had made a full attendance during the previous academic year. In accordance with national and county requirements, monthly visits to the school were made by the School Attendance Officer, whose return of statistics to County Education Offices at Wakefield had a direct influence on school funding. Registers were also scrutinised on a regular basis by the school's Correspondent, usually the local vicar or curate, who acted as a liaison agent with the school's managers and was often a channel of communication between the school, the Diocese and the Local Education Authority, the County Council of the West Riding of Yorkshire.

Comments on the quality of education being dispensed at this time by Mr Worthy and his staff of two were generally positive, despite the regular interruptions to their work caused by pupils' high absentee rates. HMI Parsons reported in 1912 that the head teacher and his colleagues were doing 'good work', though the lack of pupils staying on into Standard VII was a cause for some concern. For his part, the Diocesan Inspector, who came annually to the school to conduct pupils' Scripture examinations was pleased to conclude that the 'religious instruction [was] given with the aim of influencing the lives of the children and making them better Christians'.

A list of additions to the school's supply of readers on the eve of the First World War includes such children's classics as *Grimm's Fairy Tales*, *Treasure Island* and *Children of the New*

Forest as well as the less familiar *Hermy* and *The New Boy at Meriton*. The school was also engaged in something of a fresh air campaign at this time, acting no doubt partly on the recommendation of higher authority but also partly because of local concern that pupils' health would be jeopardised by working in stuffy classrooms. Mr Worthy records in the school log book that classroom doors and windows were 'thrown open wide' whenever a class left the room and in the upper room a child was delegated to draw the window down before going out to play. Doors were always left wide open 'during the interval'.

As events on the international stage conspired to draw Britain into involvement in a new war, it was inevitably these minor local concerns that preoccupied William Worthy and his staff. The school was now operating on a sound footing, with measures in place to secure pupils' educational and spiritual welfare in as healthy an environment as circumstances allowed. If Mr Worthy was prey to grim forebodings about the course of events in Europe at this time, no indication is given in the school log book. In fact throughout the years of conflict only one reference is made to the Great War. For Mr Worthy at least, the great unknown of 1914 was the effect which the outbreak of hostilities was likely to have on his school's planned move to the larger premises in School Lane.

9

The Village School: A century of change, 1914 - 1990

The misgivings felt by head teacher Mr Worthy that the outbreak of war in 1914 might delay indefinitely the move from Moor Lane to the more capacious School Lane premises proved groundless. The buildings which had once housed Joseph Laurence's distinguished educational enterprises and which remained the property of the Harewood Estate, now became the village elementary school, opened in time for the autumn term by the Rev Maurice Lascelles. A new chapter in the history of the school had begun.

An immediate improvement in the school's facilities was noted by a County Council Inspector later that term and by HMI Young early the following year. Each of the three divisions of the school could now be taught in a separate room, the first class being taught in two sections while more advanced scholars worked independently from books. The new rooms were described as being well lighted and ventilated and heated by hot water pipes. There was less cause for satisfaction outside the school, however, for the approach to the school was deemed to be unsatisfactory and loose stones needed removing from the playground.

September 1915 saw the school achieving a full attendance for the first time in three years, a state of affairs no doubt assisted by the return to school of little Elsie Spencer, who had been 'running wild' since February 1913. But attendance rates did not stay high for long. Stormy weather in the winter of 1915-16 deterred children from outlying farms from making the trip to school, while later in the year haymaking took its annual toll on attendance levels. Some pupils received official leave of absence, in one case 'until the end of October [1916] or the war', but more often older children, especially those nearing the school leaving of 13, simply stayed away without the sanction of a Labour Certificate in order to engage in various types of seasonal work left vacant by men called to the front. 'Poor attendance this week,' noted Mr Worthy in July 1916, 'hay making in full swing' and in October 1917 'very poor attendance this morning: 'potato scratting'.' Although the school attendance officer made one of his regular visits to the school shortly afterwards, the head teacher notes with resignation that attendance was no better for his visit. It seems that officialdom condoned if not encouraged pupils' truancy, since when he complained about the persistent absence of certain individuals Mr Worthy was informed that the magistrates would not enforce attendance. In 1918, however, pupils' energies were put to use by the school itself when it was closed for eight consecutive half days for blackberry picking. The fruit must have been particularly plentiful that year, since pupils gathered and sold 300lb of berries. Whether the proceeds of the sale went to increase school funds or were directed elsewhere is unclear.

During the winter of 1918-19 the school was closed yet again, for four weeks this time, because of an outbreak of a particularly virulent strain of influenza, which caused at least two deaths in the village. When normal timetables were resumed, visits were made by the County PE Organiser who observed pupils 'drilling', by the school dentist and by the Diocesan Inspector, who remarked on this occasion that 'it would be well if the children were able to apply the lessons of Holy Scripture to their lives more fully.'

Now at last the problem of low average attendance was to have a serious impact on the running of the school. Such low numbers could not sustain staff at current levels and Miss Waterhouse, after two years at the school, was obliged to depart, leaving only two teachers including Mr Worthy to share the work load between them. It was impossible for a reduction in staffing of this scale not to have a seriously negative effect on the running of the school and the quality of teaching it was able to provide. Problems were compounded by Mr Worthy's increasing deafness and indistinct speech, and he is remembered by one of his former pupils as being at this time a formidable, rather bad-tempered figure, wearing knee breeches and with his cane ever at the ready to punish the next unfortunate pupil.

> 'Two boys, T... and B..., have been admitted to Bardsey School. The former boy's misconduct was laid before his father who in return gave a lot of abuse. No corporal punishment was permissible as the boy suffers from a weak heart. The second boy left in sympathy with his friend.'

Extract from school log book, 1920

Miss Helm (right) 1959-60

The HMI report of 1921 noted the school's current difficulties and suggested alternative approaches by which pupils might be less dependent on direct teaching and might work more from pre-prepared materials. By 1923, however, the combination of understaffing and Mr Worthy's disabilities had resulted in the state of the school being declared 'inefficient', with pupils underachieving in all areas of their education. Finally, in 1924, after 22 years at the school, Mr Worthy took his retirement and handed over his duties to his successor, Miss Winifred Helm.

It was inevitable that Miss Helm's arrival would be accompanied by changes at the school. It was soon apparent that healthy exercise and gardening were high on the new head teacher's educational agenda. She decreed almost immediately that all children in Standards II to VII would be taken to Midgleys' field for games every Thursday afternoon, weather permitting, and that the school's stock of old gardening tools should be replaced by more serviceable ones. New ventures into Nature Study were also instituted, and villagers would grow accustomed to seeing pupils setting off into the countryside with Miss Helm at their head to examine winter buds in Harewood Avenue or to learn about plant rearing at Allison's market garden.

The wind of change occasioned by the arrival of Miss Helm was noted enthusiastically by HMI in 1925. The 'nonchalant attitude' which pervaded the school previously had disappeared and the curriculum had been broadened by the introduction of handwork and gardening. The head mistress had done 'much good work' in the short time she had been at the school. Whether the novelty of Miss Helm's new ways also had a positive effect on the perennial problem of absences is not certain, but the school log book at this period contains far fewer notes about low attendance levels than had been usual in previous years.

Visits by county health and education staff continued regularly. The drill instructor put the children through their paces or observed others doing so, and pupils must have looked forward to these visits rather more than those of the school dentist, who usually found no shortage of teeth in need of treatment. Further pain at this time took the form of annual selection tests to determine which pupils were to receive County Minor Scholarships to enable them to attend grammar school. Though numbers passing the test were never to be large, it was not unusual for a pupil or two to depart for Tadcaster Grammar School or Ralph Thoresby High School in Leeds.

The boys of 1933
Back row: A Baker, L Cowling, R Wooler, L Burnett, R Cave, M Metcalf, J Wilkinson
Front row: R Smart, W Varley, D Abram, R Ridsdale, J Linfoot, A Wooler, J Zealand

> '27 July. Very successful Garden Fete held in the Parsonage grounds in aid of the School Repair Fund. The event was supported by the Ladies' Sewing Party, the Girls' Guild, Church officials and the children themselves.'

> 'On entering school this morning, Colin Charwood got a sweet lodged in his throat. As the boy's face and neck had become very black and swollen, the Head Teacher, after trying all the ordinary first aids, sent for Dr Cook of Harewood, who after some little time succeeded in dislodging the obstruction. The boy was later taken to the Leeds Dispensary by his mother, but no further treatment was given.'

Extracts from school log book, 1936

1930 saw the introduction of the practice of distributing school milk to certain pupils whose diets were deemed to be in need of supplement. At first dried milk was used but almost immediately this was changed to Grade A liquid milk. From small beginnings such as this the distribution of school milk was eventually to be broadened to all pupils throughout the country, a practice that was to continue until the 1970s. Also new in 1930 was the annual school concert, later to become a pantomime, which every year drew large audiences, so large in fact that on occasions not enough seating was available to accommodate everyone and people were obliged to listen to the children from the school porch. That the proceeds from the concerts were donated to the Sunday School Prize Fund is a reminder of the continuing close link between the Sunday school and the day school and of the special voluntary status of the latter. The Sunday school Prize Day was an annual event, which took place towards the end of the autumn term. It was usual for the Princess Royal to distribute the prizes on these occasions, and the event would close with a short concert given by the day school children.

Throughout the 1930s reports on the school from the various inspectors continued to be favourable. HMI commented in 1933 that the scholars were tidy and neat in appearance, well mannered and that the tone of the school was commendable. The Diocesan inspector also found the school a happy place. Pupils continued to be taken out for practical lessons, to Harewood Castle, for example, with lessons on nature study, geography and social history being delivered by Miss Helm on the way. After most outings of this kind, then as now, pupils would be required to write essays on their experiences and findings the following day.

In the mid-1930s Miss Helm's creative talents turned towards the writing of plays and pantomimes for the school's annual production. The first of these was a three-act piece entitled *The Farmer's Grumble*, which was applauded enthusiastically by a large audience. Though details of the play have not survived, the title suggests that it had a local flavour, on a subject with which East Keswick pupils could identify closely. In subsequent years the indefatigable Miss Helm's productions included *Babes in the Wood*, for which she wrote songs in addition to the script and which was so popular that parents requested a repeat performance, an operetta entitled *The Rainbow Queen*, with costumes and scenery designed by Miss Helm herself, the exotic-sounding musical *Princess Ju Ju*, and the pantomimes *Jack and Jill* and *Robinson Crusoe*, in which every child in the school had a part.

The Second World War seems to have had little direct effect on the running of the school. Throughout this period life carried on as usual, with regular inspections, Sunday school prize distributions and visits from County health officials. Absences continued to be of concern, though much less than previously. On one occasion in December 1942 all three teaching staff succumbed to illness and the school Correspondent was obliged to close the school. Though it was reopened two days later on the orders of the LEA and was staffed by emergency teachers drafted in from Wetherby, few pupils could be persuaded to attend, all but six taking advantage of the situation to award themselves an extended Christmas break. Following fumigation of the premises during the holidays, the normal pattern of life resumed.

It was during the war years that Miss Helm instituted her 'camping and tramping' expeditions to the Dales and the Yorkshire coast. These holidays were for older boys and took place during the summer break, when Miss Helm characteristically gave of her own time to offer pupils what are remembered in later life by those who took part as both exhausting and rewarding experiences. Pateley Bridge was the venue for the first expedition and boys were taken from there to visit Brimham Rocks, How Stean and Fountains Abbey. Back at the school, minor crises such as blocked drains, outbreaks of ringworm and scarlet fever were offset by happier events: pupils' successes in scholarship examinations, the arrival of the school's first wireless set and the declaration by the Diocesan Inspector that the school was pervaded by a 'spirit of tranquillity' with 'prayers reverently said and hymns sweetly sung'.

During this time work had been progress at national level on a series of educational reforms which in their final form would constitute the 1944 Education Act. The measures contained in the Act, which was the work of Minister of Education RA Butler, drew together many of the proposals for a new structure for education that had been made by various committees and commissions in the inter-war years. All-age elementary schools, which catered for the mass of the country's child population throughout their compulsory education, were to be reorganised as primary schools, which children would leave at age eleven to attend whichever form of secondary school, grammar, technical or modern, was deemed appropriate for their ability and aptitude.

The Butler reforms were enacted in the summer of 1944, but the West Riding Education Committee decided to anticipate the Act's requirements by notifying elementary schools within its area that pupils who were aged 11 or over at the start of the new school year would attend one of the newly-designated secondary schools, which in the case of East Keswick meant Wetherby. Pupils were not informed of their new school until the middle of the summer holidays, a move which disappointed and angered Miss Helm. Her disapproval is noted at some length in the school log book but it is clear that she was as sad as she was angry that the LEA's precipitate move had prevented some pupils' final term at the school from being marked by one of the special occasions which she was so good at organising. Miss Helm took her responsibilities *in loco parentis* very seriously and sought to create within her school a healthy and caring community where children could develop in 'happy and helpful companionship'.

In 1945, despite economic stringencies in the aftermath of the war, the pupils sat down to a Christmas dinner of roast pork, baked potatoes, sprouts and plum pudding, followed by a distribution to each one of a mince pie and two apples. After this, Christmas dinners came to figure annually on the school's calendar of events, followed by an afternoon of games and a distribution of presents from the Christmas tree. On one occasion the day concluded by a scramble for nuts, thus ending, in Miss Helm's words, 'a happy term of hard work.'

> 'There is constant trouble with two children by the name of R ... They constantly molest, thump, kick or in other ways annoy other children at or away from school, often attacking little ones much younger and smaller than themselves. The parents take up a very strange attitude, sometimes holding the children while their boys hit them, at the same time calling the other children names which are neither fitting not polite. Of course teachers must not correct these children or a complaint is immediately made.'

Extract from school log book, 1947

From 1945 to 1950 the school continued its usual yearly pattern. Highlights continued to be pantomimes (*Sleeping Beauty* on three occasions, *Jack and the Beanstalk* and *Robinson Crusoe*) and occasional royal events, as for example in 1949 when pupils were taken to the end of Lumby Lane to see Princess Elizabeth and the Duke of Edinburgh drive past with the Princess Royal on their way to York. On the instructions of Princess Elizabeth the royal car slowed down to allow pupils to gain a better view of their future queen. The period was not without its minor crises however. To the exasperation of Miss Helm and the despair of the school caretaker, people using the school for outside events such as dances were leaving the premises dirty and damaged. Finally the caretaker, no longer able to cope, resigned her post after 28 years' service at the school. Typically, it was Miss Helm herself with the assistance of a colleague who set about cleaning the school until a replacement could be found.

Finally, in 1950, Miss Helm retired from the teaching profession having held the post of head teacher at East Keswick School for 26 years. Her time in the village had been a happy one and she had used her ingenuity and skill to enhance the education of her pupils both within and outside the curriculum.

Her immediate successor was Miss Ceridwen Lewis, whose tenure of the headship lasted only two years before she left the area to be married. In 1953, Miss EM Crosland took up her appointment. This was Coronation Year, and the event was marked at the school by the presentation to each pupil of a Coronation Mug. By this time the number of pupils on the school roll was once again small. The school year of 1951 had begun with only 24 pupils in the school, 14 in the junior section and ten in the infants. The change in status from all-age elementary to primary school was partly responsible for this decline, though the County Council Inspector noted also that a number of parents in the village were choosing to send their children to school at Bardsey, a decision possibly influenced by the poor state of the East Keswick premises. Although the larger of the two teaching rooms, housing junior pupils, was considered pleasant, the smaller infants' classroom was deemed not to offer a suitable learning environment. In addition the porches where pupils' coats and PE equipment were kept leaked, the playground was overgrown with weeds and school dinners served on plates in the school house (formerly Joseph Laurence's boarding school) were cold by the time they reached the children in the main school area. The CCI's verdict was that 'this school [could] not yet be considered a good school.'

By 1952 numbers on roll had declined to 20 and the school was facing an urgent viability crisis. Repairs to the fabric were needed immediately if standards were to remain acceptable. Responsibility for these lay with the church, under the terms of the school's

Voluntary Aided status, and in 1953 discussions opened between the Vicar of East Keswick, Rev HH Griffith, and the newly-appointed Miss Crosland in an attempt to find a solution to the problem of maintenance and repair. Finally, and undoubtedly for reasons of cost, it was judged that the school's status should be changed to that of Voluntary Controlled school. Under this arrangement the LEA would assume responsibility for the school's upkeep, though the close ties with the church would be maintained. It was not long before this change brought benefits to the school: the County Architect inspected the electrical wiring, essential repairs were carried out and in 1954 the school boiler, which had for years proved unreliable, was at last replaced. An HMI visiting shortly after these improvements was able to give a generally favourable report on the school, noting that there were now 27 pupils on roll, 20 of whom stayed on the premises for an 'appetising midday meal' and acknowledging that Miss Crosland had taken over the school 'at a difficult period in its history'.

Under Miss Crosland's headship many types of activity continued as in previous years, with the addition of some new features. The end of autumn terms was marked by carol services, nativity plays performed for parents and school parties (at one of which Father Christmas made his first appearance at the school), while church links were maintained through regular visits to the church for harvest festivals, Ascension Day services and patronal celebrations to mark St Mary Magdalene's feast day. Visits to pantomimes in Leeds now became annual events, and pupils were taken on educational outings to places of interest, for example York, Skipton Castle and Blubberhouses Moor. Royal events, such as the birth of Prince Charles and the wedding of Princess Margaret, were marked by a day's holiday.

During the early 1960s the steady trickle of pupils moving to Tadcaster Grammar School increased a little when the two-part 11-plus examination which had been used in the West Riding since 1932 was replaced by the so-called Thorne Scheme, a new selection procedure promoted by the West Riding Chief Education Officer Alec Clegg. For some years the reliability of traditional tests at 11-plus as prognostic indicators of pupils' abilities had been increasingly questioned. Moreover the restrictive effect of the 11-plus tests on the curricula of primary schools was widely recognised. Clegg's preferred alternative means of selection was the Thorne Scheme, which was trialled in the south Yorkshire town of that name and later applied to the most of the LEA area. Instead of sitting examinations, pupils were placed by their junior school in an order of merit, the top few moving automatically to selective schools and borderline cases being reviewed by a panel of teachers. Though accepted by teachers and teaching unions as a fairer system of selection, the scheme was not without its critics, who saw in it risks of favouritism by unscrupulous primary school teachers.

It was not long, however, before the issue of selection for secondary school was overtaken by events. Little by little during the decade 1955 to 1965 the tripartite structure of secondary education in the West Riding was dismantled and replaced by the comprehensive system that had been an accepted part of primary education since its inception. By 1964 14 comprehensive schools were operational in the West Riding, including Tadcaster, and in 1967 the East Keswick School log book records that pupils were leaving to attend Wetherby Comprehensive school, which, with the school at Boston Spa, would henceforward receive the bulk of children from the village whose parents opted to keep them within the state system of education.

In 1967 Miss Crosland, after over 14 years' service at East Keswick, resigned her headship. By now the number of pupils on roll had risen, contrary to all predictions, to 67. Two new 'temporary' classrooms had been erected in the school playground and various improvements to the fabric of the school had been completed, including the provision of hot water to the infants' washbasins. Despite these alterations, Miss Crosland's successor, Mr NH Graville, found the school antiquated and ill equipped, with outside toilets which were liable to freeze in winter, inadequate storage space and no staff room. Slowly improvements were made, many on a do-it-yourself basis. Extra shelving was fitted to every classroom, a makeshift office was made between classrooms in the 'temporary' block and a small corner of the main building partitioned off for use as a staff room. A solution was also found to the problems involved when the infants' classroom was required for use by the other two classes for PE, games and music lessons. By arrangement with the Village Hall Committee, these activities were transferred across School Lane to the hall, which would be used regularly until the school's final closure. For swimming lessons, pupils went first to Woodhall, from where they sometimes had to return to the village on foot because of unreliable transport, and later to Wetherby baths. So well did the children take to swimming that one year each pupil was awarded a certificate of proficiency, more than any other school in the area.

One of Mr Graville's early innovations was the formation of a Parent-Teacher Association in 1969. The Association became an integral part of school life, arranging a variety of fund-raising and social events including fashion shows, 'bargain parties', jumble sales and beetle drives. The proceeds of such events, as is usual with PTAs, were used to make up shortfalls in LEA funding, and provided items of school equipment and furnishings.

Throughout Mr Graville's headship, two strands of continuity characterised the operation of the school. Domestic problems persisted, as they had since records began in the late nineteenth century. Mr Graville's entries in the school log tell repeatedly of blocked drains, frozen toilets, inadequate heating and gas leaks. School milk deliveries were erratic, roofs leaked and such repairs as could be afforded were often badly carried out. Against the background of these problems the healthy extra-curricular life of the school continued. Pantomimes were attended, carol services held and visits made to local sites of historical and geographical interest, such as Fountains Abbey and Stump Cross Caverns. A sports day, at which East Keswick competed against Harewood School, became an annual event when weather permitted, honours being shared more or less evenly between the two schools. Royal events (the Queen's Silver Wedding in 1972 and her Silver Jubilee four years later) continued to be celebrated by the award of a whole-day holiday, while more locally the school took part in the Village Gala of 1971, an echo of the annual village feast which had been a highlight of the East Keswick social calendar many years before.

Meanwhile, at national level, legislation was being formulated which would bring radical changes to the structure of English local government. In 1974, under the Conservative government of Edward Heath, the pattern of counties and county boroughs which had been responsible for the administration of functions including education for so long, disappeared, to be replaced by larger and supposedly more efficient bodies. In the sphere of education, local authorities would be the new counties and metropolitan districts, though in view of the enormous size of many of these, the term 'local' seems hardly appropriate.

With the demise of the West Riding, East Keswick, to the dismay of many of its inhabitants, found itself in the Leeds Metropolitan District, one of the five such administrative areas which made up the new county of West Yorkshire. For some years the changeover had little effect on the day-to-day running of the school, though one immediate benefit was that individual schools were allocated allowances for minor repairs. It seemed increasingly, though, that in the case of East Keswick, nothing short of a new building was needed if the school was to conform to the operational regulations which had come into effect in 1973. In a report submitted by Mr Graville to Leeds City Council, the shortcomings of the school premises were sharply illustrated. Space available for pupils' play areas and teaching accommodation fell well below the legal minimum, as did toilet and washing facilities, arrangements for medical inspections and storage of equipment. Meals were delivered to the school from Bardsey for the 66 pupils on roll, but inadequate space was available for these to be served efficiently. There were no work areas, bookshelves or staff room for the five teachers working at the school.

Assembly of pupils, early 1980s

The final years

In the early 1970s consideration had been given to the building of a new school to serve East Keswick and East Rigton, but discussions were suspended when it became clear that future decisions on East Keswick School would soon be made in Leeds rather than Wakefield. By 1980, at a time when local government was being compelled by Westminster to maximise economies in the public services, it became clear that the LEA's vision of the school's future was conceived in terms of closure rather than reconstruction. Falling rolls across the country meant that many primary and secondary schools were operating below capacity. Redistribution of places through amalgamation of schools became a priority in all LEA areas, with the inevitable consequence that some schools would be deemed superfluous to requirements. In inner-city Leeds some seven schools of various types were identified as uneconomic, while in the peripheral area primary schools in several villages in addition to East Keswick were amongst those earmarked for closure.

Mr Graville's retirement in 1980 after a period of thirteen years gave the LEA an opportunity to review the whole issue of the school's future. Moves by the governors to initiate procedures to appoint a successor to Mr Graville were blocked, and Miss Pam Prior, at the time acting head teacher at Bardsey, was appointed to serve until the closure of the school was effected. Miss Prior was to be the last in the line of head teachers of the school, though her period of office was to prove longer than had initially been anticipated.

News of the possible closure provoked a heated reaction from parents of children at the school and early in 1981 a meeting was held in the Village Hall attended by some 40 villagers. As a first move towards mobilising opposition to the closure, a School Action Committee (SAC) was formed, which, in co-operation with the Parish Council, from which it received some financial assistance, would spearhead the anti-closure campaign. Its first step was to organise a meeting of interested villagers. In a Village Hall packed to capacity, the Chairman of the Education Committee outlined the reasons for the proposed closure of the school. Chief among these was the pressure from central government to reduce the number of surplus places in the school system, but it was argued also that significant financial savings would be made by distributing East Keswick pupils amongst schools in neighbouring villages. Despite clear opposition from villagers, when the issue of closure was put to the vote in the General Purposes Sub-Committee on 1 April, a proposal to recommend closure of the school was adopted, albeit by the narrowest of majorities.

The decision-making process was now about to enter its second stage, the submission of the Sub-Committee's recommendation for consideration by the full Education Committee. Before the Committee met, the SAC and Parish Council moved swiftly to assemble a range of arguments in support of their case. Information contained in the LEA's statements on pupil numbers and projected financial savings were disputed and councillors urged both to consider the importance of the school in the life of the community and to respect the opposition to the closure expressed by all who had been involved in the consultation process. Behind the arguments put forward on behalf of the village were suspicions that the decisions taken in Leeds had been influenced by party political considerations. The ruling Labour group on the City Council were certainly aware that East Keswick was not exactly a hotbed of socialism and may not have seen the preservation of a school in what might be seen as a largely middle class area as a high priority. Equally, though, the problem of falling rolls was a national one and pressure was being exerted by the Conservative administration at Westminster for local authorities to optimise their provision of school places.

The General Purposes Sub-Committee's recommendation for closure came before the full Education Committee on 10 April 1981. Despite the SAC's anticipation that the recommendation would be a rubber stamp issue, an extensive debate on the closure question ensued. Eventually, though, the motion for closure was passed by a majority of 15 votes to 12. Instead of accepting this decision as final, the SAC set about campaigning

The school, 1986
(Photo courtesy of Wetherby News)

with a new sense of urgency. One of its first steps was to send a 'please reconsider' notice to all councillors, while the Parish Council wrote to all Labour councillors setting out the village case against closure. The Leeds City Council meeting of 29 April, which was the last opportunity at local level for the decisions taken so far to be reversed, was lobbied by a sizeable group of villagers, who handed out 'Save our School' badges and pamphlets to councillors. Despite these efforts, the meeting remained convinced of the need for closure and the Education Committee's recommendation was approved by 57 votes to 33. A notice announcing the school's closure was duly posted in May.

The SAC now knew that its only hope lay in persuading the Secretary of State for Education not to approve the closure order, and its forces were mobilised to achieve at national level what had proved impossible locally. In September a deputation from the SAC met the Minister of Education, Baroness Young, stated their case once again and delivered a lengthy and detailed memorandum addressed to the Secretary of State for Education, Mark Carlisle. Meanwhile, in the village, a petition was organised to convey to central government the strength of local feeling and villagers were urged to write the letters of objection allowed by the closure procedures. Renewed representations were also made to Leeds City Council as a last ditch effort to persuade them to revoke their closure decision.

It was with great relief therefore that villagers learnt of an unexpected change of mind on the part of the Education Committee at its July meeting. Instead of ceasing to maintain the school, the Committee now proposed a compromise solution, whereby the school would be kept open for infants only. The jubilation of the SAC at this last minute victory was inevitably tempered by the realisation that the success had only been partial. However, inspired by the outcome of this David and Goliath meeting, the SAC resolved to continue the fight until total victory was won.

What was it that brought about this change of mind on the part of Leeds politicians? Undoubtedly the case made by the SAC and the Parish Council on behalf of the villagers was a powerful one, well presented and well argued. No support could be found in the village for the closure proposal, as evidenced by the letters and petitions which were submitted to central and local governments. Furthermore the new chairman of the Education Committee, Bernard Atha, clearly took a more moderate line than some of his Labour colleagues and was prepared to look with some sympathy on East Keswick's situation. Despite the numerous and varied representations made to Westminster, it was Atha's role at local level that turned the tide in East Keswick's favour.

The SAC continued to press for a total withdrawal of the closure notice. Local MP Michael Alison, who had lent his support to the campaign from the outset, accompanied a deputation to Baroness Young in September at the Department for Education and Science. The deputation was well received, though it was made clear that no outcome could be expected in the short term. In the interim, cabinet reshuffles promoted Baroness Young to the leadership of the House of Lords and made Sir Keith Joseph responsible for the nation's education. Scenting an opportunity to make their case directly to a Secretary of State whose constituency lay only a few miles from the village, the SAC promptly requested a meeting with Sir Keith. It was clear from Sir Keith's response, however, that he had no wish to become embroiled in a controversy which had broken out on his own doorstep and turned down the Committee's request for a meeting on the grounds that it would serve 'little purpose'.

Despite this tactical setback, the limited reprieve for the school was hailed as a 'victory for the residents of East Keswick' by Councillor Les Carter, the Conservative Education spokesman on Leeds City Council. SAC members, however, were more sceptical. Their chairman, John Priestley, was aware of the possibility that the new plans for the school might have been put forward by the LEA as a temporary measure and that total closure

Miss Pam Prior completes the school log book for the last time, July 1990
(Photo courtesy of Miss Prior)

might eventually ensue. An air of uncertainty now prevailed. Parents were unsure about which school they should envisage for their children and no measures had been taken by the LEA to approve the appointment of a permanent head teacher. By the time the new school year began in September 1982 no decisions had been made. As though to show their belief in the school's future, however, volunteers from the PTA had painted the classrooms and Miss Prior, still acting head teacher, had introduced a school uniform. For the moment at least, school life continued as before. The first computer arrived, sports events were held, new governors appointed and pupils attended services at the church.

But normal life was not to continue long. By 1983 the question of falling rolls was again on the national educational agenda, and in the Leeds LEA area it was calculated that 31,000 places would be surplus to requirements by 1989. The drop in numbers at East Keswick School from about 70 to 45 made it once again vulnerable to closure. In January 1987, as part of a consultation process, a meeting was arranged at the school between a representative of the LEA, school governors, parents and members of the Parish Council. Immediately the PTA, which now headed the anti-closure pressure group, began a leaflet campaign, urging villagers to attend the meeting and reminding them once again of the effects which the closure of the school would have on village life. By now, though, more villagers seemed resigned to closure than had been the case previously, and, despite widespread local support and renewed representations to LEA politicians and officers, the anti-closure campaign lacked the ferocity which had been so evident previously. A short reprieve was won when the Secretary of State for Education rejected the LEA's plan for wholesale reorganisation of schools within its area, but the pressure from central government for a reduction in school places was unrelenting. To the disappointment but not to the surprise of villagers, a final closure notice was issued, to take effect from the end of the school year 1989-90. All that remained was to make arrangements to mark the end of 175 years of public education in the village.

In late July 1990 a final service was held at the church followed by a farewell reception at the school. Among the guests was the Earl of Harewood, to whose estate the ownership of the school building was to revert. Miss Prior, who after 40 years in the teaching profession and ten as head of East Keswick school, took her retirement at the same time as the closure of the school. In a statement to the press, she spoke of her sadness at the fate of the school and expressed the sentiments of many when she said 'Everyone feels that the school is part of the village and village life is important. I think there are more important things in life than saving money.' The Rev Bill Snelson, Vicar of East Keswick and chairman of the school's governors, agreed, adding that if anyone was to blame for the closure it was 'the whole of modern society, which puts too great an emphasis on cost effectiveness, statistics and viability without recognising ideas of integration and community sufficiently.' Both feared that East Keswick would become 'just another commuter village, with no life of its own.'

A decade after the closure, villagers will come to their own conclusions about the accuracy of this pessimistic forecast. Growth in the village and population changes brought about by departures and arrivals during this time mean that a good proportion of present residents do not remember the school or even know it existed. Some villagers, however, still recall the pre-war days when it served the needs of the majority of village children throughout their entire period of compulsory education. Yet others remember with affection its later existence as a primary school, continuing the tradition of its elementary forerunner by being a focus for social as well as educational life and as such forming an integral part of village society, as closely woven into the community as its churches and public houses.

But times change. The case for retaining the village school, if not the arguments which supported it, was lost. Now, at the dawn of the new millennium, East Keswick children receive their education elsewhere and will continue to do so. It seems an appropriate time to celebrate the village's educational history, which had a quality of distinction far beyond what might be expected in so small a community. The development of its schools, in both the public and private sectors, closely mirrored national trends before both in turn falling victim to political and social change. This attempt to chart their respective histories may make some contribution towards giving the schools the recognition they deserve.

A note on sources

Information from a variety of sources has been used to compile this history. Parliamentary papers, official reports and census records provided much of the early material, together with Post Office and other directories available in Leeds Public Library. Previous histories of the village schools, particularly Anne Wragg's *East Keswick Church of England Infant and Junior School* (1990), were helpful and informative. Newspaper reports provided some details of contemporary events, while others were supplied through the kind co-operation of East Keswick villagers who are former pupils of the village school.

10

Transport & turnpikes

Some of the roads and tracks in the area may well predate the millennium though it is impossible to be certain since the earliest maps are much later. There is no doubt that one of the oldest is the route from Slaid Hill through Wike and up East Keswick Main Street. This is a section of a route from Kirkstall Abbey through Meanwood (Monk Bridge), Moortown, Slaid Hill to Bardsey (whose public house, the Bingley Arms, was the Priests' Inn) and on to Rigton, Collingham and York. The branch of this track from Wike and up East Keswick Main Street is described in one nineteenth century book as 'the old green lane, of old the Leeds and Wetherby road' and whilst no Roman road through Wetherby has ever been identified, this road through Wike and East Keswick follows a probable course. This suggestion, voiced by the Yorkshire Philosophical Society in 1891, is supported by pieces of Roman pottery found at Biggin, 1.2km north west of Wike. This is also the likely finding place of an altar now in the Yorkshire Museum. After passing through the village, the road may have followed Whitegate, then at the start of Crabtree Lane turning onto what is now a public footpath towards Collingham.

These roads would have been little more than tracks passable only by packhorses. Generally, the state of roads throughout the whole first half of the millennium was abysmal. From 1663 onwards this began to change with the advent of the turnpike trusts. Today these would be referred to as road building by the private sector. Private acts of parliament gave groups of local people the authority to build or improve stretches of road and to gain a return on their investment by the imposition of tolls.

By 1740, a number of trusts had been set up to turnpike stretches of the Great North Road (the present day A1 which at that time went directly through Wetherby). Over the next forty years, many other roads were turnpiked including the Tadcaster to Otley road (the present day A659 follows most of its route) through the parish under an act of 1753. Between 1796 and 1799, the tenant of the Angel Inn at Wetherby together with an attorney from the town, Theophilus Wetherhead, leased these tolls for an annual rent of £380. It cannot have been lucrative; according to the Trustees' Minute Book in the West Yorkshire Record Office they were threatened with legal action for non-payment and recovery of arrears in 1799.

The road we refer to today as the main Leeds to Wetherby road (A58) is a comparatively new road. It did not exist until the early nineteenth century. Until then, the best way to travel between the two towns was to take the Leeds to York road as far as Bramham Cross Roads, then turn north onto the Great North Road. The Roundhay to Collingham Bridge road took four miles off this route when built in 1824.

The coming of the railways

When the railways superseded stagecoaches, Wetherby lost its strategic importance in the transport network for although it was a very significant town in stagecoach days it never became an important town on the railway map.

In 1845, George Hudson began work on a branch line off his Leeds to York railway line. It was to leave it near Church Fenton on a route for Harrogate via Wetherby. By the 1860s pressure was mounting for a direct rail link between Wetherby and Leeds. The London and North Western Railway came up with one answer. In 1863 it proposed extending its line from Leeds through Wetherby to Hartlepool. Fearing an incursion into its territory, the North Eastern Railway Company, which had recently taken over the York & North Midland Railway Company to become the dominant railway company for the region, bought out the majority of the backers for LNWR's Hartlepool extension and promised new railways. One result of this was the North Eastern Railway Company (Leeds & Wetherby Branch) Act 1866.

Although this received royal assent that year, nothing happened quickly. For the *Wetherby News*, which began publishing in 1857 though not under this title, the Leeds link was to become one of its earliest campaigns and this pressure was partly responsible for it becoming an issue in the 1868 general election. The Liberal candidate was no less a figure than the chairman of the NER and the newspaper attacked him for the lack of progress on the issue. Eventually in 1876, a twelve-mile branch line was opened between Wetherby and Cross Gates skirting the eastern edge of the parish. Although built to take double track, the line was initially laid as single track. This was quite a common technique at the time. Visitors to the preserved Worth Valley Railway will see an essentially single-track line laid through bridges and tunnels built to take double track should traffic later demand such expansion.

East Keswick never had a station, the nearest ones being at Bardsey and Collingham Bridge.

At the turn of the century, this line was to gain much more importance when the route was converted to double track and joined to the Church Fenton - Harrogate line. The route was upgraded to form an express passenger route connecting Leeds, Wetherby, Harrogate and Northallerton. This necessitated building a brand new railway station for Wetherby at a different location, Linton Road. This station was on the Leeds to Wetherby section of track whereas the previous 1847 station on York Road was on the Wetherby to Church Fenton route.

There was drama on December 3rd 1902 when the 4.32pm Leeds to Newcastle express was rounding a curve near Bardsey station and the tender together with all six coaches left the rails. Seventeen people were injured, fortunately none seriously.

Local stopping services were always a half-hearted effort, but for the first half of the twentieth century this line would have been a train spotter's dream. As well as local services - some operated by steam powered autocars before the First World War - the route carried long distance freight from Teesside to the LMS network via Neville Hill and Normanton (the east coast main line had yet to be quadrupled), special excursion trains to Wetherby races - the racecourse having its own station - and even visits by the Royal train. A photograph exists of the LNWR royal train at Collingham Bridge Station in 1909, where it would be met by horse drawn carriages to convey the royal party down Harewood Avenue through the parish to Harewood House. It is thought that it made other visits, though by the 1920s when Queen Mary came, she arrived at Harrogate and was conveyed by motor car, with just freight and luggage going to Collingham.

In 1923, most of Britain's railway companies were amalgamated into four large ones. The Wetherby lines became part of the London & North Eastern Railway (LNER).

During the Second World War, the line assumed an extra importance. A secret (it never appeared on any maps before the war) Royal Ordnance factory was built at Thorp Arch, principally to manufacture bombs. Its eighteen thousand strong workforce arrived by

Bardsey Station

train, initially to Thorp Arch for Boston Spa station. As production was stepped up the number of trains needed exceeded the capacity of the line. The solution was found in a circular railway leaving the Wetherby to Church Fenton route and travelling round the site which was, by virtue of its hazardous work, spread out over a vast area. The last train ran in 1958 and the site later became industrial units and the Thorp Arch Buywell Shopping Centre.

In its final few years, the Leeds to Wetherby line was used by Newcastle to Liverpool expresses. Whilst these were steam hauled, the favoured route was through Harrogate to Leeds where the engine was uncoupled and another engine fastened at the opposite end to pull the train to Merseyside. When this service became diesel hauled it was more suitable simply to change crews, so trains were rerouted via Wetherby so that they arrived in Leeds facing the right direction.

But even this extra traffic could not save the line. It therefore became the first closure carried out under the Beeching Report as opposed to those already being planned when the report was published. In fact, the Member of Parliament for Bury defended having voted in favour of Beeching by saying that 'otherwise trains would still be running to Wetherby'.

Wetherby's case was fairly indefensible. At the time of closure in January 1964, Wetherby station alone had fourteen staff yet only thirty passengers a day. History does not record how many passengers Bardsey saw, but maybe that is just as well. With only four trains in one direction and six in the other it cannot have been many. The following timetable is taken from more halcyon days, being the November 1947 weekday timetable of the London and North Eastern Railway. SO denotes Saturdays only. There was no Sunday service. Bear in mind there would have been many more trains but only the following were timetabled to stop at Bardsey.

7.02am	Collingham Bridge, Wetherby
7.02am	Thorner, Scholes, Penda's Way, Cross Gates, Osmondthorpe. Leeds Marsh Lane, Leeds City
7.48am	Collingham Bridge, Wetherby, Thorp Arch for Boston Spa, Newton Kyme, Tadcaster, Church Fenton, Sherburn in Elmet, Hambleton, Selby
7.54am	Thorner, Scholes, Penda's Way, Cross Gates, Osmondthorpe. Leeds Marsh Lane, Leeds City
8.19am	Thorner, Scholes, Penda's Way, Cross Gates, Leeds City
8.42am	Thorner, Scholes, Penda's Way, Cross Gates, Osmondthorpe.

	Leeds Marsh Lane, Leeds City
11.00am	Collingham Bridge, Wetherby, Spofforth, Harrogate
11.12am	Thorner, Scholes, Penda's Way, Cross Gates, Osmondthorpe. Leeds Marsh Lane, Leeds City
12.40pm SO	Collingham Bridge, Wetherby, Thorp Arch for Boston Spa, Newton Kyme, Tadcaster, Church Fenton
1.02pm	Thorner, Scholes, Penda's Way, Cross Gates, Osmondthorpe. Leeds Marsh Lane, Leeds City
1.58pm SO	Collingham Bridge, Wetherby, Thorp Arch for Boston Spa, Newton Kyme, Tadcaster, Church Fenton
2.07pm SO	Thorner, Scholes, Penda's Way, Cross Gates, Osmondthorpe. Leeds Marsh Lane, Leeds City
4.20pm SO	Thorner, Scholes, Penda's Way, Cross Gates, Osmondthorpe. Leeds Marsh Lane, Leeds City
5.01pm	Collingham Bridge, Wetherby, Thorp Arch for Boston Spa, Newton Kyme, Tadcaster, Church Fenton, Sherburn in Elmet, Hambleton, Selby
5.25pm	Thorner, Scholes, Penda's Way, Cross Gates, Osmondthorpe. Leeds Marsh Lane, Leeds City
6.04pm	Collingham Bridge, Wetherby, Spofforth, Harrogate
6.23pm	Thorner, Scholes, Penda's Way, Cross Gates, Osmondthorpe. Leeds Marsh Lane, Leeds City
7.05pm	Collingham Bridge, Wetherby, Thorp Arch for Boston Spa, Newton Kyme, Tadcaster, Church Fenton
9.30pm	Collingham Bridge, Wetherby, Spofforth, Harrogate

Bus services arrive

The railways lost out to road traffic, which as far as public transport was concerned meant buses. In 1925, the Wetherby firm of Riley and Hawkridge began a bus service to Leeds via East Keswick. The bus terminus in Wetherby was the Town Hall which was used as a turning round point, and a return ticket to Leeds cost 3/6d (18p). It quickly faced competition from the Roadcar company which took it over in November 1927. Two months later this company was renamed West Yorkshire Road Car Co Ltd and the village bus service was to remain in its hands for the next sixty years.

The route has remained largely unchanged, though many buses went much further than Wetherby. Some continued to Harrogate via Spofforth, some to Knaresborough via Kirk Deighton and three a day continuing to York via Long Marston. The Leeds to Wetherby section followed the A58 between Leeds and Bardsey Bank Top. Here it split, and for most of the century roughly half the journeys deviated via East Keswick and Linton (as service 39 once route numbers were introduced), and the other half staying with the main road to Wetherby and on to Knaresborough as service 40. Interestingly, the timetable point within the village shown in the 1932 bus timetable is 'City Square', an unofficial name used by the villagers to describe the junction of Moor Lane and Main Street. That year the fare from the village to Wetherby would be 4d (1½p), whilst Leeds would cost 9d (4p) single or 1s4d (6 ½p) return. As a matter of interest, a ticket from there to London was 16/- (80p) single, 26/- (£1.30) return. The village bus service was operated, through necessity, by single decker buses until the removal of the low railway bridge at Keswick Lane in Bardsey.

By the end of the century, the route was in the hands of First Bus, who had taken over most of the municipal services of Leeds before absorbing many of the Leeds area services of West Yorkshire Road Car. If anything, this gave the village a better bus service as every bus on the service followed the same route from Leeds through Bardsey Bank Top and East Keswick not splitting until Collingham where roughly half returned to the

Local bus heads out of the village for Leeds through a flooded Main Street in front of Brooklands

A58 past the Barley Corn Inn as service 98, the others travelling via Linton as service 99. Many evening and weekend buses, being subsidised by the local authority, were extended to Kirk Deighton on the West and North Yorkshire boundary, fulfilling an obligation to provide an evening bus service to that village.

There have been two other public bus services through the parish. A route from Wetherby to Otley before the Second World War operated by a Mr Thornton before being taken over by Samuel Ledgard and extended to Ilkley, and in the 1990s a local supermarket began a free bus starting in the village to Asda at Killingbeck each Friday morning.

Sources

Bus services, from *Whatever the Wetherby* by G R Stead

Railways, from *Railways around Harrogate* trilogy by Martin Bairstow

National Railway Museum archive material.

Turnpikes, from *Wetherby, the history of a Yorkshire market town* by Robert Unwin

North Eastern Railway Company (Leeds & Wetherby Branch) Act 1866

West Yorkshire Road Car Company Timetable 1932

11

Notable houses

This chapter is based upon replies to a questionnaire circulated to all appropriate residents as part of the research for this book and our thanks are due to all who participated in the exercise. It is supplemented by information from *East Keswick Remembered*. The houses included are those on the Ordnance Survey map of 1892.

The approximate number of houses in East Keswick was as follows:

1796	Harewood Survey	55
1811	Census	61
1821	Census	61
1831	Census	70
1851	Census	88
1861	Census	101
1871	Census	108
1881	Census	115
1891	Census	113
1999	Electoral List	480

As can be seen there have been at least 367 houses built in the village since the 1891 census. We say 'at least' because several rows of former cottages have been converted into single houses (e.g. Wellington Place) and some cottages have been demolished (e.g.

An early photo of the junction of Main Street and Moor Lane

Moor Lane Cottages built 1758). With the exception of the Travellers Rest and outlying farms and cottages, the only houses in East Keswick in 1851 lay along Whitegates, Main Street, School Lane and Moor Lane. Cleavesty Lane and Lumby Lane did exist but there were no houses on them. The development was entirely linear and there was no infill between the radial roads. Additionally many of the houses that existed then have been substantially modified and thatched roofs have entirely disappeared. Thus what we now think of as East Keswick is largely the creation of the last hundred years.

Whitegate

The cottages on the right hand side at the top of Whitegate are built on a plot of land that did not belong to the Harewood Estate and which was originally called 'Elliker'. The Cottage has a well in the back garden, vaulted cellars and was probably built around 1670.

Hillside was built as a Primitive Methodist Chapel in 1847 and became a private house around the turn of the nineteenth century. The arched windows at the side and back probably reached floor level when it was a chapel. A plaque by the front door records its origin.

Greenfields was built around 1850 and has changed its name three times. It was originally called Daisy Bank in 1909 and Shamballa in 1933. When it was sold in 1909, its owner was John Midgley, a family name that occurs frequently in property ownership in East Keswick.

Mount Pleasant Cottages were in existence in 1851. On the 1892 O.S. map the cottages are marked as the Post Office. Although *East Keswick Remembered* states that they were originally known as Middle Cottages, it is tempting to relate them to the Mount Pleasant mentioned in the 1851 census as the home of Joseph Sawer, butcher and schoolmaster and Riley Sawer his son. Before Ashfield was built opposite, Mount Pleasant would have enjoyed a beautiful outlook, giving some reason for its name. In the 1881 census a Riley Sawer is recorded as the owner of Ashfield and it would seem that the house was built about this time, as there is no mention of it in the 1871 census. If the identifications are correct, Riley Sawer, in the course of his life, moved from one side of the road to the other.

East Ings was formerly two cottages occupied by William Midgley whose initials were visible (1975) on the gateposts 'W.M. 1876'. The house is said to have been one of those where Methodist meetings took place.

Dains Corner in the early 1900s

Main Street. Note the thatched roof

The bungalow, Green Row, occupies the site of a former pair of cottages at right angles to the road and of which two walls still remain flanking Whitegate and the passage leading round the back of Ingle Nook.

Ingle Nook is said to have been stables at one time. There were cellars beneath what are the gardens whose arches can still be seen on the wall flanking the road.

Ingle Nook was partly obscured by a cottage built onto Wayside Cottage of which the roofline can still be seen on the gable end. This now defunct cottage was replaced by Mr Bolton's house also demolished but clearly visible in a pre-1916 photograph.

Wayside Cottage was originally two properties with kneelers on the roof. There is another vaulted cellar beneath it with a well. These cellars are said to be similar to ones in Thorner in which flax was dried. The Dains family ran a shop from here before moving into premises opposite, which became a hairdresser's, and finally to Central Stores, now the end house of the Ingle Nooks.

Main Street

Wray's Cottage is another old village property still without running water or electricity in 1975 according to *East Keswick Remembered*. The clock on the wall outside is both a village landmark and the source of much discussion in the Parish Council minutes. As can be inferred from the sign visible in old photographs, it was once a shop selling sweets. There are 'Harewood Fans' above the windows. It was in the Wray family for three generations and before that was a draper's shop.

The Old Forge, as the name implies, was once a smithy and dates from the early eighteenth century. It then became a decorator's shop before becoming the Post Office and then a private house.

Ryder Cottage is thought to have been built in the mid seventeenth century but has been repeatedly altered over the years. Originally it was two thatched cottages and owned by the Dawson Charity. There used to be a draper in one cottage and a wheelwright in the other.

Below Ryder Cottage there used to stand a substantial thatched cottage which must have extended across the road which is now The Close.

Orchard Cottage looks from the plans as if it was one side of a square enclosure with

Ryder Cottage on Main Street

Stocks Hill was so named because it was the site of the village stocks

The Old Parsonage

Orchard House, Orchard Barn forming two other sides while the fourth side was made up of buildings now demolished but shown on the plan, giving the whole the appearance of a farmstead. However if this were to be the case, it must be ancient as there is no record of the site being a farm in the recent past.

The Old Parsonage was also originally a farm - Low Farm - and was built around 1690. As one faces the house, the section to the right is the original house to which the left section was added in 1860. The older part was originally thatched. Unusual are the five pane windows and hammer beam roof on the original. There are also original shutters throughout the ground floor. There is an old well at the rear, an arched cellar and a dairy at the side of the house. The barn/coach house/garage in front of the house with its blocked entrance shows the original height of the road before the road was lowered at Stocks Hill. When St Mary Magdalene church was built in 1856, it became the

Jessamine Cottage, once a slaughterhouse. The man is Mr Mead

designated clergy house but, according to *East Keswick Remembered,* was never popular with the curates on account of its size.

Proceeding down Main Street there were a number of dwellings now demolished on the site of Argyle Mews and the pair of semi-detached houses Briardene and Elmwood. One of them housed Illingworth's the butchers.

Winton House was built shortly after the Laurence Memorial Chapel and was the home of Charles Midgley until his death in 1910. Who lived in the house until his executors sold it in 1932 is unclear as no further deaths are mentioned. The land which accompanied the house was farmed by the Illingworths and sold to the Dysons in 1962.

Jessamine Cottage is in two parts. The older single-storey part dates from 1690 and was used as a slaughterhouse at one time. The two-storey upper section is Georgian and there is a well in the yard at the back. In the Harewood sale of 1950, Jessamine Cottage is described as 'an attractive small holding with land extending to $11^{1}/_{2}$ acres'.

Darley Cottage was until 1967 the village Post Office with Mr Darley the Postmaster. The house probably dates from 1750 and was thatched at one time. The presence of an

Darley Cottage was once the village post office

old barn adjacent and a large well in the garden suggest that it may have been a smallholding.

Clitheroe Cottage and South View appear on the 1851 map. They were both sold in the Harewood sale of 1950 when the tenants are listed respectively as Miss Ridsdale and R Illingworth Limited.

School Lane

The Moons built Laurel Bank in 1861 as a grocer's shop and currant store. Originally Mr Moon traded from West End Stores before building Laurel Bank. He had a considerable grocery empire with a number of branches. The three-storey building must have dominated the entire area and certainly has the look of one of the old West Riding

View of Laurel Bank around 1910 and 1970

mills. The upper floors have been converted into flats.

Laurel Dene was built in 1790s and used to be the home of the village cobbler. The Old Mill was built in 1792 as the original Methodist Chapel and was subsequently used as a flourmill until 1916.

Hopewell House is built onto the back of the Old Mill and was certainly in existence before the Laurence Memorial chapel was built in 1891 as it appears on the 1848 survey and therefore was in existence when the Old Mill was still a Chapel. There are no windows at the rear and the walls are thick.

Clitheroe House and School House formed the school that the Laurence family ran from around 1820 to 1890. School House has a well in the cellar and another in the garden. There are brick arched cellars and the rafters still have the tree bark on them. The house was reattached to the school when the village school moved there in 1914. It is said that after Joseph Laurence's death the property reverted to the Harewood Estate and later to the Church. The present owner gives the date of School House as 1690.

North View is Georgian and belonged to the Harewood Estate until 1950. Originally it was a farm and was composed of two cottages as evidenced by the floor construction. It was converted into one dwelling in Georgian times. The roofline was much lower as can be seen on the east wall. The doorway on Moor Lane was an addition in Georgian times to balance the frontage of the building. Evidence of its former life as a farm is provided by the outbuildings which until recently contained three milking stalls, a pigpen, loose boxes and a hen run. The house has undergone many alterations but still contains some Georgian glass in its windows. There is a pump in the yard and a covered-in well. It was bought by the tenants at the Harewood sale. These were the Watson family who ran a carrier's business and hired out landaus and waggonettes.

Moor Lane

West End Cottages were built about 200 years ago as homes for the workers at Manor Farm. The whole row has undergone considerable modification over the years as evidenced by the change of the roofline and the traces on the walls.

One-Up One-Down Cottage at the top of Church Drive is claimed to be the oldest surviving building in the village and dates from around 1700. More recently it was converted for use as a garage. But the interior still contains many original features -

Moor Lane Cottages dated 1758, but now demolished. Those in the picture are (left to right) Mr Dains, Mrs Carrick's father and Mrs Ridsdale

Moor Lane

fireplace, Yorkshire sliding window, floorboards held in place with wooden pegs and a wooden plank staircase. It has a pantiled roof and distinctive chimney composed of four flagstones. The present owner has embarked upon a careful restoration.

Darwent House was built around 1870 as the home for the headmaster of the school which forms the side of the block. The school transferred to School Lane in 1914 when the property became the Men's Institute. Presumably Darwent House became a private residence at the same time. It was sold as part of the Harewood Estate sale of 1950. The Men's Institute eventually was incorporated into the Village Hall as a snooker club in 1985 and the property, like Darwent House, became a private residence.

Church View Cottage was built 1800 - 1820 and was part of a block of three. At some

One-Up One-Down Cottage

stage the bottom two furthest away from the road were knocked into one. There are no foundations; the walls are simply built on large stones set in the ground. The walls are sandstone with a slate roof (which may originally have been stone). There is a stone enclosure in the garden which was the toilet block for the three cottages. At one time the Hardistys and Ridsdales occupied them. Presumably they were built as cottages for farm labourers.

Nearby was a row of cottages pulled down when Moor Lane was widened.

Ivy Grange (called Ivy Cottage in the 1950 Harewood sale) is recorded as early as 1759. It is believed that it was originally single-storey. One of the interior beams came from a ship and there is an old stone fireplace. It was in the possession of the Wright/Barber family for many years. It is described in the sale catalogue as follows: 'Ivy Cottage stands well up overlooking the Valley of Keswick Beck'.

Moat House is said to have been built from the stones which comprised the moated mansion to the rear of the existing house demolished in the seventeenth century. The house was a farm and the outbuildings included a piggery, hen loft and a cattle barn with

Craine Cottage

Moat House from Keswick Beck. Early 1900s.

a beautiful cantilevered staircase leading up to the hayloft. A brick-lined well in front of the house has been filled in for safety reasons. In one of the garden walls there are three bee boles (recesses in a wall to keep bee skeps dry). A former resident at Moat House was Harold Wilton who was George Formby's dresser.

Old Hall Farm is another property reputed to be built (as its name implies) from the stone of the old manor house. It is said to have been built in 1780. Along with Manor House Farm it was sold in the Harewood auction of 1950.

Hope Cottage is the end cottage of what originally was a block of four cottages with Craine Cottage at the opposite end. It is believed that Hope Cottage and its neighbour were originally stables while Craine Cottage was a farm. The whole block predates 1750, but the window structure (as seen in a pre-1900 photograph) suggests a seventeenth century date. The upper windows were Yorkshire sliding windows. The whole series of properties has undergone considerable alterations. It is believed that they were originally part of the Harewood Estate but they did not form part of the 1950 sale.

Cleavesty Lane

Linden House/Elm Bank/The Mount and East Mount are linked together by the purchase of three acres of land by George Laurence from John Sharper in 1835. At that time none of the above houses was in existence. George Laurence built The Mount and East Mount as one property sometime between 1835 and his death in 1859. Whether he built it as a residence or as a school is unclear. However by 1859 The Mount was an academy for young ladies run by the Misses Laurence. The building is not recorded in the 1851 census when George Laurence and Mary Laurence are recorded as living in Clitheroe House. Presumably the house building must lie in the period 1851 - 59. In 1869 Mary Laurence bought the whole property and land from her family and remained there until her death in 1899. By this time the house had been divided into two, Mary Laurence occupying The Mount nearer to Cleavesty Lane and George Moon occupying East Mount. The date of the building of Elm Bank/Linden House is confusing. On the 1851 Ordnance Survey map there is a substantial house marked on the spot where the present houses stand. Yet a sketch map shows the land in question owned by Mary Laurence and William Laurence, her brother, with no sign of the houses. Although there is no date on the sketch, it is unlikely that Mary and William would be mentioned if their father, the owner, were still alive. Hence the sketch ought to postdate the death of

George Laurence in 1859. The present owners believe the house was built around 1856.

Public Houses

There are three public houses in East Keswick and all three have existed for many years - years in which the population of East Keswick has trebled. Were our ancestors thirstier than their descendants?

Both the Duke of Wellington and the Old Star are shown on the records for 1822. At the back of the Duke of Wellington were the stables for Moons the grocers and at one time there was a blacksmith's shop at the lower end of the yard.

The Old Star was originally a farm. In the 1851 census, it was kept by Abraham Barrett who lists his occupation as innkeeper and butcher. However in the 1861 census his

The Duke of Wellington as it appeared in 1965

occupation is given as butcher and farmer. Obviously he could have changed occupation and residence but one wonders whether the Old Star was permanently a pub or varied according to the vagaries of trade or even the landlord's social inclination. However, The Old Star was sold by David Midgley to the Tadcaster brewery in 1889.

According to the present landlord the Travellers' Rest is marked on a map of 1640. Its site and name derive from its position at the top of the rise out of Collingham on the haulage road from Tadcaster up Wharfedale. The earliest mention we have found is 1771 when Joseph Midgley bought the inn and later sold or leased it to Christopher Smith and Joseph Clafton. In 1830 Robert Midgley repossessed the property because money was still outstanding and it stayed in his family until 1913. Robert himself was the publican until his death in 1843, at which time his widow Sarah took over until her death in 1869. Their son-in-law then became landlord until his death in 1913. Thereafter a legal wrangle ensued with two branches of the family claiming the inheritance - Tindall v. Tindall. It remained as a 'free house' until 1934 when it was sold to Ramsden's Brewery of Halifax. In 1965 the Tetley brewery bought out Ramsdens.

The field opposite the Travellers' Rest used to contain the village bull pound. It was marked out by four stones which were engraved BTL, for Bull Tethering Land.

Acknowledgements

Mrs Joan Frankland
Carlsberg Tetley Brewery Archives
Dr OS Pickering, Brotherlon Library Special Collections

12

The village expands

In 1822, the *Baines Directory* gives the population as 296 and lists the key inhabitants as John Clough, lime master, Thomas Dean, wheelwright, Thomas Flint, innkeeper of the Old Star, George Lawrence, schoolmaster, James Midgley, boot and shoe maker, George Parker, butcher, Robert Scatchard, stonemason, John Scatchard, surgeon, John Sharper, maltster, William Teale, lime master and Abraham Wormald, victualler of the Duke of Wellington.

The nineteenth century was the beginning of the major expansion of the village. Some of the implications - its church, school and railway - are dealt with in other chapters. One of its first modern businesses had its roots in 1861 when a Mr Moon built the large three-storey building on the corner of School Lane and Main Street, the beginning of an empire that would extend to eleven branches.

Mr Moon began as a tea blender and hawked tea. He then had what became known as Little Moon's Shop on West End, and later moved to Laurel Bank where he ran the grocer's store and currant house. Drays were used to convey stock between branches and the stables were behind the Duke of Wellington Inn. The houses known as The Orchards were built for employees and for several years they were provided with electricity by an oil powered generator at the back of Laurel Bank. Brooklands was another development instigated by the business for its employees. When built, at least one workman resigned after the footings were completed, being concerned about the muddy state of the ground so close to Keswick Beck. Until the end of the nineteenth century the road forded the beck close to this point. Audrey Dawson used to live in the

School lane showing Moon's mill, around 1910.
(Photo courtesy of Dr Helen Greysonand J B Simpson LLB)

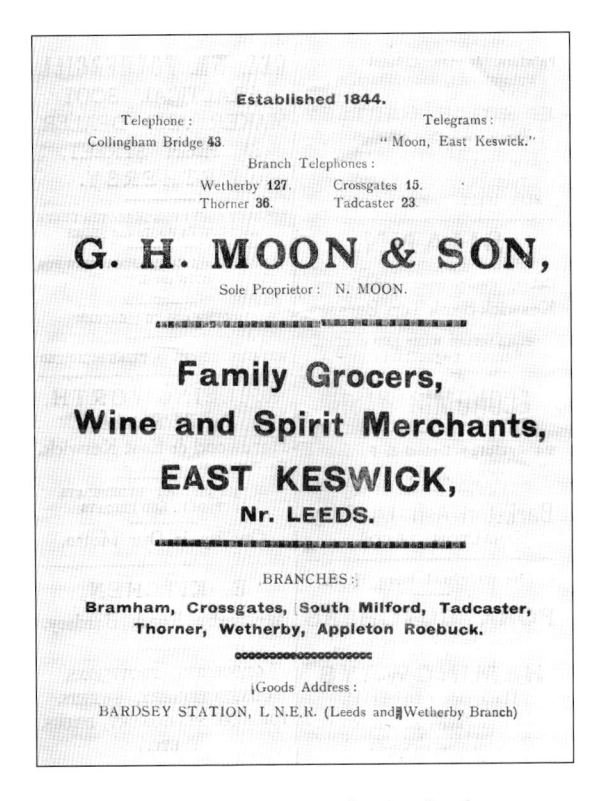

```
                    Established 1844.
      Telephone:                    Telegrams:
  Collingham Bridge 43.         "Moon, East Keswick."
                  Branch Telephones:
              Wetherby 127.    Crossgates 15.
              Thorner 36.      Tadcaster 23.

          G. H. MOON & SON,
              Sole Proprietor: N. MOON.

              Family Grocers,
        Wine and Spirit Merchants,
              EAST KESWICK,
                  Nr. LEEDS.

                    BRANCHES:
      Bramham, Crossgates, South Milford, Tadcaster,
          Thorner, Wetherby, Appleton Roebuck.

                  Goods Address:
      BARDSEY STATION, L.N.E.R. (Leeds and Wetherby Branch)
```

An early Moon's advertisement

cottage adjoining the Duke of Wellington and can recall hearing the horse in the stables kicking during the night. This area behind the Duke was known as the Paddock, the name which would later lend itself to a nearby development. Frank Moon himself lived in a large house at Harehills Avenue in Leeds.

Eventually the upper storeys of Laurel Bank became flats and the grocery business continued under Dunhills until 1968. For the final years of the millennium, the retail premises were used as Jonathan Crawford Interiors.

Parish Council

Shortly before Christmas 1894, the village adopted powers made available by local government statute to begin its own parish council. The council was to comprise five -

Brooklands, with the footpath across Blacksmith's Field to Bardsey in the foreground, taken around 1920.

later to become seven after the Second World War - unpaid councillors elected every four years. The first council comprised John Burnett as Chairman, James Firth as Vice Chairman and joint overseer, John Richard Johnson, James Midgley as overseer, and Robert Brelsford as treasurer and clerk for the following year. Early meetings were held in councillors' homes and the first parish meeting, a public meeting where the council reports its activities to the village, took place in the church schoolroom the following March. Within a year, all meetings were being held in the schoolroom and the policy of having a paid clerk was established by J W Neal being appointed at a salary of one pound per annum.

By the time that the councillors were due to stand for re-election in March 1898, the council was clearly popular since no fewer than seventeen names were proposed for the five positions. However, twelve withdrew to save the expense of holding a contested election.

The concerns of the council changed little over the years. Complaints about litter, rubbish and public transport feature almost continually in its records. One of the most emotive subjects regularly discussed was street lighting. From 1896 onwards, satisfaction was expressed at the cost saving by not having street lighting. The subject came to a head in 1977. The newly opened roads The Paddock and Paddock Green were due to have seven street lighting columns under the policy of the recently formed West

Brooklands

Yorkshire County Council. A census of village opinion revealed that 77% opposed lighting, many believing that not having it added something to the village's charm.

War

Today, it is hard to conceive of any catastrophe which would rob the village of more than one in seven of its able bodied men, but such was the effect upon East Keswick of the Great War and perhaps the reason why this small community remembered its dead in not just one, but three separate memorials.

George Allison was a market gardener from Moor Lane, close to its Harewood Avenue junction. Samuel Asquith lived in Plum Tree Cottage on Moor Lane. Henry Barber lived on a smallholding on Moor Lane; his family had been in the village for hundreds of years. Barber's Bottoms, the only safe swimming spot on the river, bore their name. Frederick Eustace Brearley lived at The Orchards; Eric William Brodrick lived in Brooklands having recently married into the Moon family. Herbert Sanderson Dains was from the family shop on the corner of Whitegate and Main Street. Ernest Dalby lived on West End. Charles Hardisty's family had been in the village since 1676. His father was Chorister and Churchwarden at St Mary Magdalene and Charles lived on Whitegate,

Village rooftops in the School Lane area around 1910.
(Photo courtesy of Dr Helen Greyson and JB Simpson LLB)

four doors below where the War Memorial would be built. Thomas Edwin Johnson, a joiner, lived on Whitegate, Laurence Longfellow was his next-door neighbour. Edgar Sawyer lived at Ashfield on Whitegate; William Worthy was the schoolmaster's son. Harold Rushforth lived at The Travellers' Rest. William Stanley Johnson's family had been in the village since they took Old Hall Farm in 1841. Arthur Phillips, Edgar Sampson, Herbert Thackray and John Percival Wade completed the death toll of eighteen from a village of only 462. We have no records of the injured or maimed.

As far as we know, all those mentioned fought in the West Yorkshire Regiment whose composition included the Leeds Pals. Ernest Dalby lost his life at the Somme in September 1917. Frederick Brearley died of his wounds in June 1920; he was 33. Thomas Johnson was 30 when he died. Lawrence Longfellow, an only son, died in France in October 1918. He was nineteen years old. Charles Hardisty died the day after the armistice was signed.

They were brave men too. Longfellow, Phillips, Rushforth and Sampson were awarded the Military Medal, Edgar Sawyer the Military Cross.

The first commemoration of their sacrifice was the planting of the avenue of lime trees which still stand on Crabtree Lane. Initially sixteen were planted, presumably before the death toll rose further, each bearing a small varnished wooden plaque dedicated to one of the fallen. On January 31st, 1920 'in not very propitious weather conditions' the Reverends Lascelles, Scott and Harrison in the presence of 'a goodly gathering of residents and sympathisers' dedicated this avenue to their memory. The Parish Council maintains its upkeep.

A year later the stone war memorial was erected. It took the form of a Celtic crucifix four and a half metres high designed by the East Keswick War Memorial Committee who raised its £207 cost by public subscription. It was unveiled on October 8th 1921 by Colonel Lane-Fox.

The third memorial is a wooden lychgate with pitched slate roof which was added to the entrance of St Mary Magdalene Church in 1922. The church had made efforts to support the West Riding War Fund and the Belgian Relief Fund during the war.

Between the wars

Life could not be the same again, but it was still an idyllic rural lifestyle between the wars as many villagers and ex-villagers have testified. Mrs G Mooney of Exeter grew up in the village in the 1930s and 1940s. In these halcyon days when cars were rare and horses, traps and carts the main form of transport, most villagers had an allotment and grew their own vegetables and reared their own pigs and poultry. Milk was collected in pails and nearly all able-bodied villagers were involved in getting the harvest in.

The days between the world wars were untroubled times remembered by ex-villagers with affection as a heavenly childhood. 'We played on hollows near Harewood Avenue (opposite Cleavesty Lane) we called The Cleaves. A footpath led from here to the river past a spring. We swam at Barber's Bottoms where the footpath met the river and younger children paddled at Sandy Beach, between here and the footbridge. The flat ground nearby was used for camping by the army or territorials and the scouts. It was the army that built the steps from here to Ox Close Wood.'

Empire Day, May 24th was known as Royal Oak Day in the village according to ex-villager Jessie Harris and a peculiar tradition took place. Girls had to wear an oak leaf for school that day or 'the lads would be likely to nettle our legs'. The tradition of Oak Apple Day is one commemorated around various northern dales but more usually associated with May 29th to mark the day when Charles II entered London after England had been a republic under Oliver Cromwell. The involvement of oak leaves denoted the fact that Charles concealed himself in an oak tree following his defeat at Worcester. Church services would be held that day, children would expect a day off school and boys would chase children who had forgotten to wear oak leaves and nettle their legs, the day also being known as Nettle Day.

Until 1934 there was no provision in the village for cover by a fire brigade, no refuse collection until three years later, and no regular dustbin collection until after the Second World War. Before the arrival of mains water, the village was served by a number of pumps. Those who did not have their own water supply used the Low Well Pump. The parish council erected its notice board on the site in Main Street during 1975. Other pumps were located at The Old Star, The Cottage on School Lane, Keswick Beck Bridge, Church Drive fields and over a sink in Clitheroe Cottage

May 6th 1935 was a day of celebration in the village commemorating King George V's Silver Jubilee. His death a year later was followed by the abdication crisis but the coronation of King George VI on May 12th 1937 gave the village a chance to celebrate again. Both these special dates followed a similar pattern. The village sent a telegram to their majesties the King and Queen: 'Loyal greetings and a long and happy reign from the villagers of East Keswick, Yorkshire'.

An open air service at Stocks Hill started the day followed by a procession round the

One of the village water pumps, in this case the Victorian pump outside the Cottage, School Lane made by Richard Stead of Thorner. (Photo from a series taken around 1910 by kind permission of Dr Helen Greyson and JB Simpson LLB.)

village, down to the beck bridge, back to Stocks Hill, along West End to Old Hall Farm and back, up The Mount, down Clay Lane and up the village to the cricket field which was then located next to Lupton's Farm. The procession was instructed to be as quiet as possible passing the war memorial in respect to the fallen of the Great War. The May Queen was crowned at 1pm, and children's sports followed at 2pm. The ubiquitous Miss Helm was there to organise maypole dancing, pillow fighting for boys, potato races, sack races and boys' wrestling. Prize giving was followed by a comic cricket match and teas. Every person over seventy was presented with a walking stick or tea caddy. There was folk dancing in the early evening, followed by adult sports which included a donkey race and slow bicycle race, an award for the best-decorated house, and a whist drive. Those still in the party mood could then enjoy a dance in the schoolroom until 1.30am.

The West Riding County Council marked the occasion by presenting each child in the

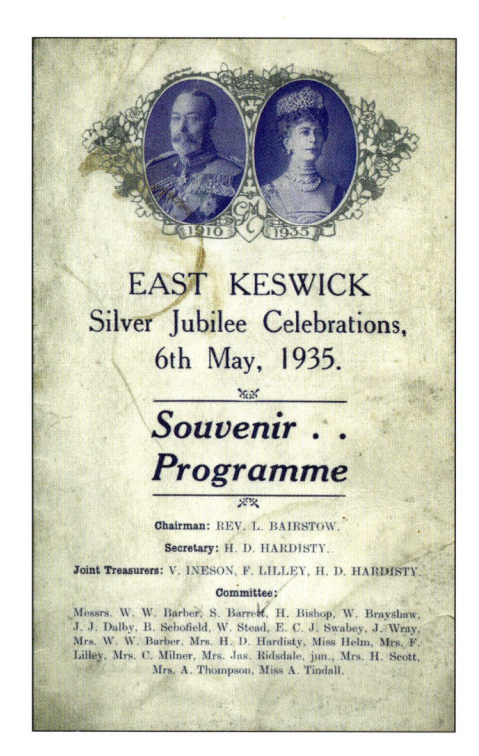

Cover of 1935 Silver Jubilee programme

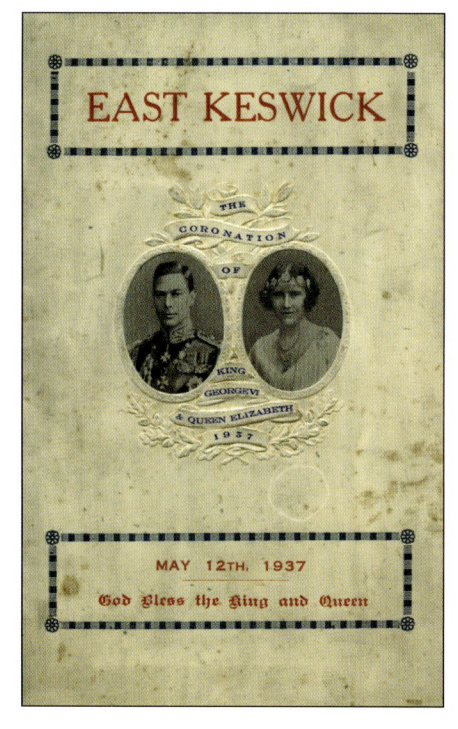

Cover of 1937 Coronation souvenir programme

village with a gift. Girls received a silver teaspoon from A W Marks, The Headrow, Leeds 1. Boys got a penknife.

War comes again

Betty Moscrop recalls the day Britain declared war: 'It was a Sunday in September. Mr Chamberlain said if Hitler had not replied at such a time we would be at war. Our family had been blackberrying at Wike and Bardsey and collected fourteen pounds of berries. Mum said if she was going to make jam we would have to do without sugar in our tea. We heard the sirens and saw searchlights at night but didn't really understand, only being ten years old.

'Miss Helm, our head teacher, got us to knit mittens and balaclavas in khaki and air force blue wool for the forces. We also had some evacuees in the village. There was Joan and Ian Jeffries and their mum who had been bombed out in London. They came to Mr and Mrs Wormald who lived next door to us. Also Mrs Hardesty had two children from Leeds. One was Helen Kaufman and a boy called Kingsley Peach.

'Dad went to work at Thorp Arch which was a factory making munitions. He cycled there every day and still tended three allotments and the field and animals.

An early photo of Stocks Hill

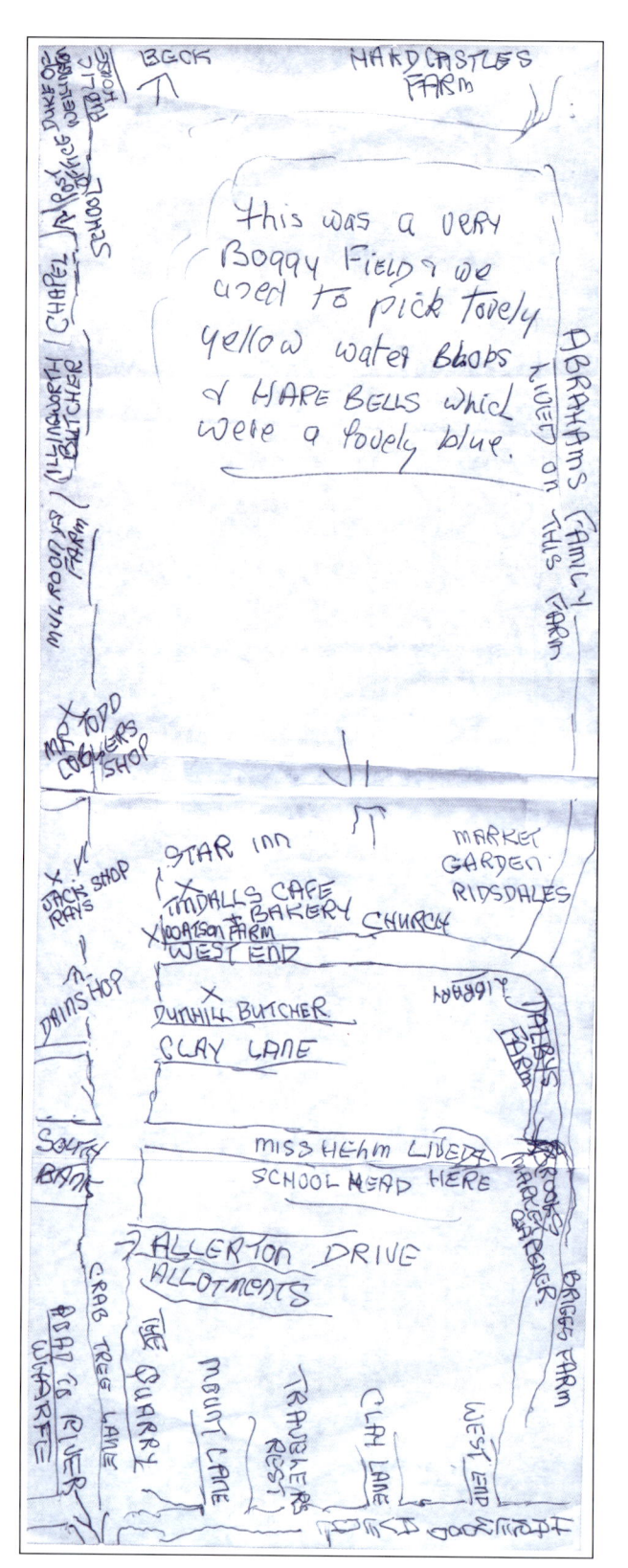

The village as remembered from childhood by Betty South (née Moscrop)

'My sister Jessie went to tea with the Princess Royal and it was very exciting when she planted a tree at the war memorial. She was the lucky one whose name was pulled out of a hat by a member of the Parish Council.

'We always went to the cricket match on Saturday afternoons and on Whit Monday we had a party and races in Illingworth's field near the school. Children from a school at Hunslet also came and they loved it. We had garden fetes and our mum got first prize for teacakes, we were so proud. Jack Howarth a timber merchant (the man behind Howarth Timber of Leeds) lived next door to the parsonage and he donated a big breadboard and rolling pin which I have passed on to one of my daughters.

'We spent a lot of our summer four weeks holiday paddling down at the river. It was lovely near the bridge and the water was very clear with lots of little fishes. People used to come from Leeds in motorbikes and sidecars. On summer Sundays a man used to come to the village on a bike with a large box from which he sold ice cream. On it was written Stop me and buy one. All twelve of us used to have a halfpenny cornet. That stopped at the outbreak of war.

'I left school at fourteen. My twin and I passed a scholarship to go to Pitman's College but our family couldn't afford the uniforms at that time so we did not go. I worked at Tindall's Café going with Henry delivering bread and a few cakes around two or three villages as far as Scarcroft.'

The village Home Guard had their headquarters at the Toc H building just inside the grounds of the Old Parsonage. Amongst the platoon was Audrey Dawson's father whose wartime job was building Lancaster bombers in Leeds. The Old Parsonage was also the first aid post where Miss Wilkinson, a retired nurse, taught first aid once a week, sometimes enacting mock air raids with casualties. She owned some furnished cottages up Whitegate which were popular as first homes for village girls.

There were a number of German and Italian prisoners of war working on local farms. They were brought in each morning by army trucks from Scotton near Knaresborough, Wetherby Grange and Scarcroft and collected at the end of the day. Most spoke good English as D Suttle remembers: 'we worked together and could converse with them. They were never any trouble and all were quite good workers.' Her sister remembers working alongside two German POWs called Werner and Gehrhardt. 'As schoolchildren we were allowed two weeks holiday in the autumn for potato picking. This was lucrative work for children, earning them five shillings a day. They were most considerate to us schoolchildren and lifted up our full buckets of potatoes onto the cart'. In 1945 she joined the Women's Land Army and was sent to Lincolnshire. Her

The young man delivering to Ryder Cottage is Derek Illingworth

family, the Moscrops, were the largest in the village during the war years. The family had moved from Wike when there were nine children in the household and this later became twelve. They lived at 6 South Bank and their father rented a field near to the Travellers' Rest where they kept a pony, goats, two pigs, hens and occasionally geese. Betty recalls going 'sticking' on Saturday afternoons which meant collecting kindling. The children enjoyed helping their father to collect and empty dustbins at sixpence a time. The bins were emptied in a pit off Crabtree Lane.

Miss Helm, the school headmistress, wrote and produced a pantomime each year frequently attended by the Princess Royal. She was Mary, sister of King George V, who had married the then Lord Harewood, a man fourteen years her senior. The princess and Miss Helm were good friends. One ex-villager, Audrey Dawson, recalled the visits of the school dentist who took teeth out in Miss Helm's kitchen.

Despite an air raid, this January 1943 panto at Bardsey went on. The cast was (back row) F Stead, B Oveton, E Richardson, M Mulrooney, J Wolstenholme, M Ripley, J Mellor, M Richardson, (front row) Mrs Copley, S Lazenby, J Richardson, Mrs Scott, M Vacher, Miss Smith, Mrs Moon, P West, Mrs Blackburn, J Tipple

Summer 1941 brought an outbreak of ringworm to the village. Many children including six of the Moscrop family had to have their heads shaved. The same year there was an outbreak of scarlet fever and the school had to be fumigated along with many homes. Six Moscrop children were hospitalised at Thistle Hall Fever Hospital, Knaresborough, for six weeks. Visitors could only see them through the windows and their mother caught two buses to do this. Their dad cycled there. Jean was there for four weeks, a period that included Christmas. She remembers that Miss Helm filled a stocking for every East Keswick child at Thistle Hall.

At the end of each term Miss Helm would throw sweets to the floor causing a mass scramble of excited children. Whenever the school inspector came, the children either sang *Jerusalem* or recited *Vitae Lampada* by Henry Newbolt. Other popular poetry was *Sea Fever and Cargoes* by J Masefield, *Leisure* by W H Davies and *Daffodils* by Wordsworth.

There was no doctor in the village. The nearest was Dr Cook and Nurse Watson and both lived at Harewood. The Moscrop family paid tuppence a week to a healthcare scheme but their mother was excluded, as she was diabetic. The family had to pay twenty pounds for her care, a small fortune at the time.

Miss Helm was the treasurer of the East Keswick Hockey Team. The school children played hockey at the top of Dalby's field behind the library. They were classified as PE lessons.

Miss Helm would invite Princess Royal and her lady-in-waiting to school concerts. The princess always looked quite comfortable sitting on the row on the headmistress's chair with a cushion and blanket. The boys would always enjoy the cricket matches against Harewood boys in which Lord Harewood and his brother The Hon Gerald would play.

The Princess Royal suggested that the village girls get together and join the Girls' Training Corps. They were taught Morse code, map reading, semaphore, car maintenance, how to cook cheese scones with dried egg and to bake date and prune cookies.

Whilst learning first aid at Harewood House they were invited to have a cup of tea with the Princess that she made herself on a small stove using a silver teapot.

The Air Training Corps was also based at Harewood and the village boys would cycle there each week for training. Jessie recalls that they always felt safe with these lads escorting them home after the dances they attended at Harewood School. The Princess would also attend for an hour or two. As teenagers they would also attend dances at Collingham Village Hall and occasionally visit the cinema in Wetherby, though that entailed missing the last five minutes of the film in order to catch the last bus home.

The Princess was also present when the village pantomime *Babes in the Wood* was performed in Bardsey during an air raid.

The Second World War was to cost the village five more good men. John Mitchell lived in Whitegate, Lawrence Wright in Moor Lane. Harry Seekin lived just above the Parsonage. He was a gunner in the Royal Artillery who lost his life in August 1941. Reginald Johnson lived at Hollin Hall; he was a driver in the Royal Army Service Corps when he died in February 1945, after the fall of Germany and just months before the end of the conflict. Miss Helm too was to be bereaved: William Veseley, the other villager killed, was her nephew.

After the war a small piece of land known as Little Burton Close was given by Edmund Patchett to the parish council as a War Memorial Garden and garden of rest to be used by the public forever. Mr Howarth donated the trees and the conveyance of the land took place on November 14th, 1949.

'Princess Rosebud' pantomime, 1947. Our picture shows the cast which comprised, left to right (back row) Eileen Moscrop, Michael Naylor, John Lister, Ann Betts, Mary Greaves, David Tuck, Carole Garbutt, David Gray and Geoffrey Cowling. Middle row 'fairies' were Wendy Cowling, Arlene Cooper, Dorothy Burnell, Patricia Betts and Rosemary Wilkinson. The front row shows Michael Yates, George Dalby, Peter Nettleton, Yvonne Watson, Margaret Nettleton, Malcolm Cook, Colin Burnell, John Hotson, Olive Yates and Michael Cowling. Michael Naylor and Ronnie Burnell (who is not in the photograph) left the village as teenagers on assisted passages to Australia.

Peace returns

One post-war year Miss Helm took a group of girls camping to Pateley Bridge which they reached on the back of Mr Varley's lorry. School swimming lessons were novel, to say the least. Without any access to school swimming baths Miss Helm taught swimming strokes to children laid across chairs. Once proficient in this art they walked down to the River Wharfe where after a little guidance they swam across the river and back.

Miss Helm also taught ballroom dancing at the 'village hops' where she also played the piano.

The school Christmas pantomime of 1947 was *Princess Rosebud* which was performed also at the Royal Ordnance factory at Barnbow. Eileen Moscrop can still remember the excitement of dragging the background curtain down from the attic of the schoolhouse

Owen Bowen - still painting at 92 years old

and later being able to help Mary I'Anson to repaint it. Mary taught at Tadcaster Grammar School and was an artist of some repute and featured frequently in an Anglia Television series. She would often include village schoolchildren in her pictures if they watched her paint. She was not the only artist in the village. Angus Rands and Owen Bowen were two others of note. The actress Madeleine Vacher who appeared on many radio plays taught elocution from her home opposite Dalby's Farm.

This was to be the last year of pantomimes at the school as the following year the village hall had opened. Eileen and others drew hundreds of tickets for the opening to be sold at a shilling each.

Eileen remembers life existing around the school and the churches. She went to the Methodist Sunday School and remembers lantern slides in winter. There would also be beetle drives and rabbit pie suppers at these evening guild meetings for teenagers as Jessie Coote remembers. Miss Phyllis Hayes from Bardsey was the superintendent there for many years, walking to the village and back twice each Sunday for morning and afternoon Sunday schools.

Miss Helm always made a fringe for the harvest festival pulpit, wheat, oats and barley being donated by Mr Dalby. She also organised dancing round the maypole and Jubilee Day events at the village cricket ground in Lupton's field. The children spent long summer evenings playing rounders and cricket on the backfield behind the grove or in the cowslip field which was near Park Mount. Summer days were spent at the river swimming at Barber's Bottoms and usually they walked from the river and up Crabtree Lane, then walked back up through the field to the Cleaves calling to fill up their water bottle at the spring. Winter days would be spent sledging in Mulrooney's field.

The Bramham Hunt met regularly at the Duke of Wellington and at the entrance to School Lane. The children were allowed out of school to watch them head off, often including the figure of the Princess Royal looking very regal in her black coat and tall black hat.

The village was a popular destination for camping trips as Doris Thompson, then Lambert, of Leeds remembered 'When I was about fourteen, I went with the guides to

The Bramham Moor hunt met twice a season in the village.
(Picture by courtesy of Mrs Kellet and JB Simpson LLB)

The hunt begins, heading out of the village up Main Street. (Picture courtesy of Derek Illigworth)

camp for one week at Dalby's Farm. It was a lovely experience. The guides were from St Clement's Church in Chapeltown Road which is no longer there. The son of the farmer who helped us a lot was called John Dalby. I still enjoy going through East Keswick, it is a lovely visit'.

Around this time a village football team was formed. However 'East Keswick Tigers' soon met their match when they played the tall navy cadets from The Ship in Wetherby.

From Village Hut to Village Hall

In October 1944, the villagers of East Keswick decided to raise money for a 'Village Hut'. By the end of that year £89 11s 4d was in the bank. Over the next three years, fund-raising by the East Keswick Little Theatre, WI Christmas Fair, and assorted jumble sales, dances, garden parties and donations had taken this total to £655 16s.

Activities at this time took place in the school and the aim of the fund-raising committee was a village hall to be proud of. By 1946, plans had been drawn up. The following year, the committee was offered a temporary building, free of charge, through the National Council for Social Services and other bodies, for a rent of thirteen pounds a year. A public meeting was held and it was decided to accept this offer and use the money raised for furnishings. The temporary village hall was to be utilised for fund-raising for a permanent hall and positioned in such a way as to allow the permanent building to be erected alongside. In 1948, Lord Harewood gave the site to the village.

From the following year the temporary building was in full use. Funds raised were increasingly being needed to pay for the running costs of this building and the dream of a new permanent village hall was receding.

It was not until the mid sixties and until the village was expanding that serious fundraising could begin to make inroads into the amount required. If the village could raise a quarter of the cost, the West Riding County Council would match it and central government would add the other half. Before this could be achieved, The County Council was abolished in the local government reorganisation of 1974 and the authority which would take responsibility for the village - Leeds Metropolitan District Council - had no grants available. More fundraising was the only answer and many galas, barbecues, auctions, nearly new sales and prize draws followed.

The Village Hut, predecessor to the Village Hall

BUCKINGHAM PALACE

13th July, 1977

Dear Mrs. Lupton,

    Thank you very much for your letter of 10th June enclosing a copy of the East Keswick Souvenir Programme for your Silver Jubilee celebrations.

    I have shown this to The Queen and Her Majesty was both very interested to read of the events that were arranged and also greatly appreciated your good wishes for her Silver Jubilee year.

    Yours sincerely,

Mrs. Lupton

Letter from Buckingham Palace

In 1979, an extra building - called the Supper Room - was added to the first. By early 1984, with funds at £84,000, it was decided to go ahead with the new building, even though a loan would be needed to complete the project. After much consultation with the Sports Council, who were providing a substantial grant, the Yorkshire Rural Community Council and many other sources, architects' plans for the permanent hall were drawn up and the steel structure erected in August 1984. A local builder handled the main building work with some ancillary work undertaken by exterior landscaping provided by the Manpower Services Commission.

The village commemorated the Queen's Silver Jubilee in 1977 with a church service, bonny baby competition, children's fancy dress, election of Miss East Keswick, gala stalls, sports events and evening bonfire with fireworks.

The loan to complete the project was provided with the backing of the Parish Council and was to be paid back over a period of twenty years. The first event in the new Village Hall was a United Church Service in February 1986. The old temporary hall was then demolished to make way for the car park. One of the most memorable events from the early years was the live transmission of the BBC Radio 4 programme 'Any Questions' which took place in November 1989. On the panel were Mo Mowlam, later to become Secretary of State for Northern Ireland; Norman Lamont, later to become Chancellor of the Exchequer under prime minister Margaret Thatcher and one of those later responsible for her demise; David Marquand who was Professor of Contemporary History and Politics at Salford University; and novelist Janet Cohen, a director of Charterhouse Merchant Bank. In the chair was Jonathan Dimbleby.

Housing battles

In the latter half of the twentieth century, the village came under external pressures to expand. The rapid increase in car ownership made East Keswick an attractive commuter village for Leeds and surrounding towns. The first shot in this battle was fired in 1958 when a village landowner, Lucy Linfoot, announced that she was planning to sell eleven acres of pastureland for building. She told an astonished village that she had submitted an outline planning application in respect of area south of Moor Lane as far as Keswick Beck.

Local feeling was so strong that it led to a public meeting and the creation of the East Keswick Rural Preservation Committee. If the group was expecting the backing of Wetherby Rural District Council they were to be disappointed. Wetherby supported the

Illingworths' Farm, 1963, showing the paddock which later gave its name to the road built on the site

idea of building on eight, if not all eleven, acres.

The application came to the attention of the Minister of Housing and Local Government who ordered a public inquiry in July 1959 under Mr D J Offord. Offord concluded that not more than twenty houses should be built on that section of the area north of the public footpath but left the door open for future development south of this line. His report said that development of the whole site would be harmful to the character and development of the village and the number of houses allowed was to keep the development in line with the density of the time.

The housing developer Wimpey bought the land and submitted a detailed application for seventeen houses which were subsequently built forming Church Drive. A year later, Wimpey submitted a further application on an outline basis to develop the remaining five and a half acres. But this was to be refused on the grounds that it was too soon after the first development for the effects of it to be seen and that there was a possibility of the land being included in the Green Belt.

Wimpey appealed but without success. In April 1962 the minister decreed that any further development south of the public footpath would be suburban development into pleasant countryside and result in a cul-de-sac of excessive length. He also thought it would be a mistake to alter the rural character of the village by encouraging its development on any appreciable scale as a dormitory community.

Wimpey would not take no for an answer and applied again in summer 1963. They were refused again for much the same reasons. The East Keswick Rural Preservation Committee could be disbanded.

Seven years later West Riding County Council published a Village Plan which designated East Keswick as a settlement of significance in which only limited development should take place.

A period of relative calm ended in 1971 when Wimpey submitted a detailed application to build forty-five houses. A public meeting was called and the Society for the Preservation of East Keswick was formed to coordinate the village response. A public inquiry heard that the existing sewerage and sewage disposal facilities were operating

Stocks Hill & Main Street, 1920s

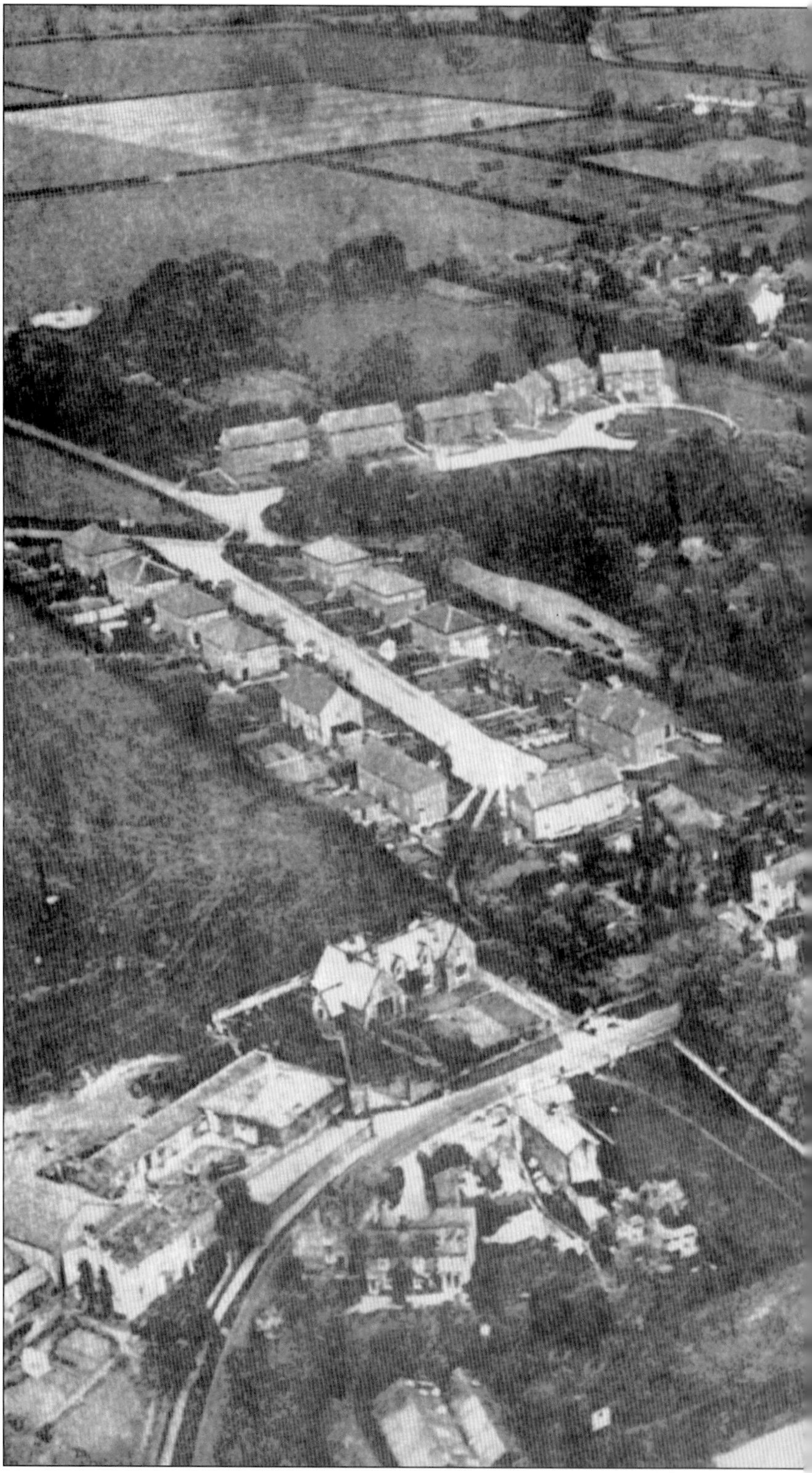

East Keswick 1956

near maximum capacity and could not cope with accepting and treating the additional effluent that such a development would create. Wimpey were to lose again, but undaunted submitted a further application several months later on a reduced scale of thirty-eight dwellings. This time Wimpey were to be turned down not just for the earlier sewerage reasons but also because some of the site was being considered for future educational needs and that as the Secretary of State had already said no twice there had to be a substantial reason to persuade him to change his mind.

1974 saw a major change in English local government. Leeds Metropolitan District Council was formed and this led to improved consultation with the Parish Council on planning matters. Quite quickly, a large part of the village was designated a conservation area including the appeal site.

In an attempt to overcome possible objections Wimpey asked for permission to build a temporary sewage treatment plant linked to Keswick Beck. Fate intervened in January 1975 with an outbreak of salmonella in the village and though no link was ever found between the infection of cattle and the polluting of the beck, it became another reason to oppose the application. Wimpey lost again, partly because it was believed that granting the proposal would lead to the proliferation of small sewage treatment works in similar areas.

A year later Yorkshire Water offered to improve the existing sewage works. The village suspected Wimpey's hand in this and it was later found the house builders had contributed fifty thousand pounds to its cost.

Another inquiry and another rejection for Wimpey followed, but this time the Secretary of State said he saw no objection to the development if the sewerage difficulties could be overcome, an adequate road layout achieved, and an application more appropriate to a rural village than an urban housing estate put forward.

Encouraged by these comments, Wimpey sought discussions with Leeds planners and put forward an application for seventy-five houses. Local feelings reached new heights; especially as such a development would have been much higher in density than the twenty-four persons per acre proposed by the Village Plan. The chairman of Leeds City Council Planning Committee presided at a crowded, and hostile, public meeting in the Village Hall. Residents complained that the Wimpey plan would increase the number of houses inside the conservation area by 37^{1}/$_{2}$%.

Eventually the extension to Church Drive was built and marketed as The Belfry but the village had scored a major victory reducing the number of houses built from seventy-five to a mere thirty-two. The luxury five-bedroom detached houses were priced at

£150,000. But within a year of the last house being sold, Wimpey's next development in the village at Keswick Grange were selling for a hundred thousand pounds more. A Wimpey spokesman told the *Yorkshire Evening Post* at the time that although the houses had similar specifications, Keswick Grange homes were bigger even though these had the same number of bedrooms. The huge increase in price was mainly due to a nationwide housing price boom and the popularity of the village's locality that placed East Keswick in the middle of the sought-after golden triangle of Leeds, Harrogate and Wetherby. Villagers had started to become more aware of the value of property in the village from 1977 when a derelict cottage on Main Street reached £9,800 at auction. This cottage had been lived in until the previous year by a recluse whose only amenities were a cold water tap, primus stove and hurricane lamp.

When Keswick Grange was completed, Wimpey announced that they had no plans for further development in the village.

Conservation area status and VDS

The village was designated a conservation area in 1974 by the then newly-formed Leeds Metropolitan District Council. In his recommendation, the Director of Planning wrote that this was 'to preserve its character and control development. It is considered a fine example of an old farming village, consisting of tightly developed, pleasant small stone properties and includes two churches, a Church of England school and two public houses'. The boundary of the conservation area covers the whole village from Keswick Beck to beyond Lumby Lane. The Parish Council commemorated its centenary in 1994 with the publication of a booklet on the village history. By this time, planning applications formed a significant proportion of its workload. It described its function as 'to institute, maintain and improve benefits enjoyed by inhabitants of East Keswick' paid for by a separate small precept on the community charge. At the end of the millennium its officers consisted of Dr Sylvia Pinkney as Chairman, June Gallant as Clerk, with councillors Andrew Batty, Ralph Carr, Gordon Nutter, Melanie Smith, Eddie Tinsley and Janet Thornton.

One of the final significant events of the millennium in the village was the creation of a Village Design Statement. Recognising the need to limit development if the village was to retain its unique identity in the future, a public meeting held in October 1997 resulted in the establishment of the Village Design Group. The aim of the group was to write a Village Design Statement, a document which would sum up the characteristics of the village which it was hoped developers would respect in any proposed expansion of the village. It was therefore not a pressure group against development but rather recognition that if development was inevitable then it was better to preserve the local character through guidelines than to allow unrestricted growth. The group liaised with Leeds City Council's planning department and involved the Parish Council, Countryside Commission and as many residents as it could. In November 1998, an exhibition at the Village Hall attracted wide interest. Photographs and maps drew attention to particular local features and asked visitors to complete questionnaires on what they liked, and did not like, about the village. More than three hundred were completed and six hundred comments put forward which ultimately formed the basis of the statement.

Sources

Yorkshire Post Newspapers archives
Mrs D Suttle of Wetherby
Mrs Eileen Wright of Pool
Jessie Harris of Derbyshire
Audrey Dawson of Otley

13

Wildlife Trust

The village is probably unique in having its own Wildlife Trust, a village-based charity which owns and manages considerable tracts of lands within the parish boundary. This remarkable achievement had its origins in the 1990s and the vision of one man, founder member David Smith.

David had lived in the village for over forty years and observed many changes in the local environment including the loss of woodland and flower rich pastures, the draining of wildlife-rich wet meadows and the removal of hedgerows. He believed that this, combined with intensive use of farmland, had resulted in the loss of hitherto common farmland birds and a negative effect on wildlife. David decided to do something to protect the remaining areas of wildlife-rich land in the area and, through the village newsletter, sought others with similar views.

The result was a meeting in April 1992 which formed a Wildlife Group to care and manage areas of wildlife interest in the parish. A committee was elected and a constitution adopted. Soon after, the group applied to become a charitable trust with the aims of safeguarding wildlife and natural habitats by acquiring and managing sites of local, regional and national importance and by encouraging landowners to include conservation as a criterion in land management.

One of the first campaigns was to purchase Ox Close Wood, a thirty-five acre woodland close to the River Wharfe which had recently gone on sale. Ox Close had many plants indicative of ancient woodland and was one of the most important deciduous woodlands in the region. Lying partly on the edge of the magnesium limestone belt and containing

In May 1992, villagers were invited to walk Ox Close Wood and to consider getting behind the fundraising project

both acid and alkaline soils and the associated flora suited to either, it is rich in species. Its trees include ash, oak, elm, field maple, small leaved lime, spindle and dogwood. In spring, it is carpeted in bluebells giving way to yellow archangel, cowslips, primroses, stitchwort, dogs' mercury and wood anemones creating a vivid tapestry of colour. In summer, it is one of the few areas where the rare parasitic thistle broomrape is found. Roe deer, foxes, badgers, noctule and pipistrelle bats are just a few of its animals, whilst the river attracts heron and kingfisher. Green, greater and lesser-spotted woodpeckers all frequent the woodland.

In the seventeenth century, Ox Close had been part of the village common land. Then known as New Close, it was a grazed wood where village freeholders could graze horses, cattle and sheep. Each person was allowed to take wood from allotted areas provided it was for local use. Those accused of breaking this rule could be taken before the Harewood Manorial Court, as indeed two were in 1751 and fined one shilling and sixpence (8p) each.

As pressure mounted to enclose remaining open land, a note scribbled on the back of the 1799 village survey observed 'the common pasture, or rather wood called New Close is well stocked with hazel and other wood and it is a great pity it cannot be kept shut up'. Two years later it was and became the private property of Harewood Estate

Bird box making was one of the many regular activities organised by the Trust

and later sold on to the Harewood Sawmill. It was the sawmill that had put it up for sale in 1992 but the £25,000 asking price was feared to be beyond reach.

In May, interested local people were invited to walk the paths through the wood and experience the woodland flowers in full bloom. The beauty of the area captivated those who took part. One local supporter generously offered to back the Trust with a large donation towards the purchase price. When the Trust used its charitable status to claim the tax back through Gift Aid the purchase could become a realistic goal.

Other generous donations followed from local residents and Leeds Birdwatchers, Leeds Urban Wildlife Group, Leeds Naturalists and Scientific Association, and Esmee Fairburn Charitable Trust made it possible to put in a firm offer and by March 1993 the Trust was the owner of the largest woodland in the parish.

By this time the Trust had identified Keswick Marsh, a six-acre area of wet pasture opposite the Duke of Wellington as an area of interest. It was a type of habitat becoming increasingly uncommon as almost all wet pasture in surrounding countryside had been drained, treated with herbicides and re-seeded to increase agricultural productivity. A decision was made to approach the Parish Council with the offer to look after the area and request a small grant towards its care. This was accepted and the Marsh is now one of the few examples left locally of a semi-natural wet pasture with an accompanying rich flora and fauna. Three ponds were dug to increase the area of permanent water and a rich diversity of wetland wild flowers can be found there including marsh valerian, meadowsweet, water figwort, water mint, marsh marigold, greater salad burnet, amphibious bistort, water avens, lady's smock and ragged robin. Large numbers of common frog breed here as well as two species of uncommon snails, one a rare freshwater variety.

The area became the Keswick Marsh Nature Reserve and display boards were erected to tell visitors what to look out for, not simply amongst the flora, but amongst the wetland creatures encouraged to thrive in this peaceful haven.

The fourth piece of land that the Wildlife Trust were to take responsibility for was a small redundant limestone quarry and associated field behind the war memorial on Crabtree Lane. Known as Frank Shire's quarry, the land was in the ownership of the Parish Council and, as with the case of Keswick Marsh, the Trust was to agree terms with the council for its upkeep. The meadow is one of the few uncultivated pastures left in the parish.

Within eighteen months of its launch the Trust was to have sixty local families and individuals in its membership and a secured a modest annual grant from the Parish Council. Membership was to double by the end of the millennium thanks, in part, to an imaginative programme of events. Mini beast mornings were held in the Village Hall, pond dipping for children took place at Keswick Marsh. River surveys, bird and bat box making days, tree identification days, fungi hunts, orienteering, treasure hunts, animal tracks and signs recognition, dawn chorus walks and dormouse surveys were just some of the ways the Trust were to entice villagers to care about their wildlife heritage. Children played a large part in these events and the annual bluebell walk was a popular part of the village calendar. Local schools have carried out surveys on Trust land, Brownies have worked towards conservation badges there, evening campfires have been held in Ox Close Wood by Cubs, whilst Rainbows and Beavers have learned how to make string from nettles and soap from horse chestnut leaves there. Teenagers have worked towards their Duke of Edinburgh awards with the Trust and most villagers have had the chance to buy the charcoal it has produced from trees felled in the wood for effective conservation management.

Managing so many acres of rough pasture without resorting to mechanical mowing required a natural solution and so, in the mid 1990s, the Trust bought its own livestock. A Shetland sheep, two Hebridean sheep and two goats were the initial stock used, and were highlighted in a survey for the Grazing Animals Project. GAP was seeking to advise

The Wildlife Trust produced charcoal from its felled trees which was sold in outlets in the village

others on the most effective use of animals and grazing methods for conservation management and the information gained from East Keswick made the Wildlife Trust a pioneer of this type of management regionally.

Trust volunteers have given thousands of hours to conservation efforts. In conjunction with the British Trust for Conservation Volunteers they have added or repaired gates and stiles, cut steps, erected fencing and planted hedging.

By the end of the millennium the Trust had played a part in national initiatives, such as cultivating the once common Black Poplar. It had also undertaken wide-ranging surveys of trees and hedgerows throughout the village. It provided a stimulus to the care of the countryside felt far beyond the forty plus acres of rich wildlife habitat it presided over. The East Keswick Wildlife Trust had become a unique and highly prized asset of a distinctive community.

14

A vibrant social scene

One of the oldest continuous village societies is the East Keswick Snooker Club. It was originally part of the old Village Institute based in Moor Lane opposite the church and was in operation well before the First World War. Earliest surviving records relate to 1915 when the annual subscription was 2/- (10p) and half price for soldiers. From time to time parcels were sent to soldiers at the front. Smokers received an allocation of cigarettes worth 1/8d (8p). Non-smokers received a tin of foot compound costing 3d, a 4d stick of shaving soap, sixpence worth of chocolates and an Oxo Trench Heater worth 6d.

The Institute was a place where men could play darts, billiards and dominoes. It also formed the village library which was open on Thursday evenings with a William Parker in charge. This was very much a men's (and lads') institute. Although girls were allowed in to choose books, if their choice was not considered suitable reading for an under sixteen then it had to be changed for one that was.

The Institute remained open throughout the war. In 1935 a caretaker was appointed who was paid 5/- (25p) per week plus free firewood. The club remained popular until it was closed 'owing to war circumstances' on September 18th 1940. The Home Guard was granted use of the premises during the war's darkest days. When it reopened in 1943, the annual subscription was 3/- (15p).

At the 1947 annual general meeting George Robert Holdgate-Booth, already in his 35th year as President, was re-elected and remained in office for a further five years, a final total of forty.

East Keswick Men's Institute

In 1950, the building was purchased from Lord Harewood for five hundred pounds. On October 16th 1957 Michael Rowlands was elected as a junior member of the Institute. In 1965, it had a membership of thirty and opened Monday and Wednesday afternoons from two till five, then Monday, Wednesday and Saturday evenings from 7.00pm till 10.30pm. Its minutes thanked Mr Dyson for the 'generous gift of a toilet and washbasin', and Mr Dalby for 'connection to his supply', stating that now it had toilet and washing facilities. Having served on the committee for many years he was elected Chairman in 1975 and was in office when the decision was taken to sell the building which became a private dwelling house. £20,000 from the proceeds was used to purchase a room in the new Village Hall, the rest being spent on furnishings, fittings and two championship standard snooker tables. The club was renamed East Keswick Snooker Club. At the end of the millennium the club was in use seven days a week and subscriptions were £18 per year, with a reduced rate of £10 for the over 65s and students.

Sport

The age of the East Keswick Tennis Club is a matter for some debate but a Member's Rule Book from 1924 shows it to be fully active then. Its official title was the East Keswick Lawn Tennis Club as it began on grass courts. It has, however, always been in the same location, close to Carr Green. The membership fee in 1924 was five shillings per year and its aims were to provide a facility for anyone in the village who wanted to play tennis at recreational and 'club' level. It rented its land from Harewood Estate and at the end of World War Two was paying five shillings a year each Lady Day. In 1949, along with many other tenants of the Harewood Estate, the Tennis Club was offered the site which it bought the following year for £75.

Club records show there were periods when membership, particularly of male players, was low. In earlier years there was an active social side to the club and funds were raised by dances. Friendly competitions were held against Bardsey and Collingham tennis clubs.

There was once a hut on the site which was replaced by a pavilion in 1958. The original site had courts on two pieces of land though one was later sold to the Parish Council to provide an area for children. In 1994, with financial assistance from the Foundation for Sport, the two current courts were built and the surrounding land given over to the Parish Council following the relocation of a public right of way.

By the end of the century, the club had a thriving membership exceeding one hundred, amongst them children, many of whom received professional coaching.

Another sporting body which had its roots around the same time was the village Cricket Club. Formed in 1920 it won the Wetherby & District Cricket League in its first full

Cricket field on Crabtree Lane

Cricket team around 1935

The cricet team win the Coronation Cup in 1957... again!

season. In 1937 the league held a special knockout competition to commemorate King George VI's coronation, and the village team won that too. This Coronation Cup is still presented annually to the first or second eleven player with the best match-winning performance. During the period 1953 to 1962, the club won the league no fewer than six times.

The Legion

After the First World War, an organisation which was to have a major role in every part of the country was the Royal British Legion. The Bardsey and East Keswick branch became part of the larger Collingham and District branch which covered those three villages as well as Linton and Wike. It was commonly supposed that the Legion was only for ex-service people but in truth it welcomed all those who simply supported its aims.

Nationally, its most visible role was that of extensive benevolent work, financed in part by an annual poppy day appeal, where paper poppies, resembling the poppies of Flanders Fields from the First World War, were sold. Local fund raising was particularly concerned with three residential and nursing homes, four convalescent homes and a specialist medical centre for ex-service personnel. The local branch had especially strong links with the Lister House Residential and Nursing Home in Ripon, including the adoption of a residents' room there.

At the end of the millennium, the branch was thriving. With a record number of eighty members and several social functions ranging from barbeques to sausage and mash suppers, outings and coffee mornings, the branch was very popular. Central to its calendar was the annual act of remembrance at the village war memorial.

The Women's Institute

Another society with a long history was the East Keswick WI. The National Federation of Women's Institutes was formed in 1915 with the aims of offering opportunities for all women to enjoy friendship, to learn, to widen their horizons and together influence local, national and international affairs. On November 12th 1940, weeks after the Home Guard had taken over the Village Institute, fifty-nine East Keswick ladies met in the schoolroom to form the East Keswick Women's Institute. All WIs belong to the National body and a County Federation. East Keswick became part of the Yorkshire Federation until county reorganisation in the 1980s moved it to the West Yorkshire Federation.

The WI trip to The Potteries in their 1958/9 season

Whilst every decade provided opportunities and challenges, the Sixties and Seventies stood out. Membership rose to over a hundred and the multiplicity of talents generated participation in national and county competitions.

To commemorate the silver jubilee of the national federation in 1965, East Keswick WI compiled a scrapbook entitled *A year in the life of the village*. Twelve years later, to mark the Queen's Silver Jubilee, a further national competition inspired a second scrapbook. A huge amount of historical research had taken place two years earlier for the European Architectural Heritage Year. The East Keswick submission reached the finals of the competition and went on public display in York. A short while later the material was displayed in East Keswick Village Hall where it was very well received. One overheard comment that it should be a book resulted in just that, the publication of a 1975 booklet *East Keswick Remembered*. In pre-computer days this involved a tremendous amount of work and seven hundred copies were subsequently sold at 55p each.

The profit from this enterprise financed a collage for the entrance of the Village Hall in recognition of East Keswick WI's fortieth birthday, many of the buildings being sewn on by their inhabitants.

The WI was the first body to start raising funds towards the original hall, a temporary building erected in 1949 which was used as a base for fund-raising for a permanent structure. Over the years members continued fund-raising for the maintenance of the old building and efforts were redoubled in the Sixties and Seventies to raise funds for the new hall.

In the early seventies, a group of villagers asked Wetherby Council if they might have a Flower Arranging Class in the Village Hall. When the answer was that no funds were available, the group asked the Village Hall Committee if they might have use of the hall if they found their own teacher. So began the East Keswick Flower Club which has been in full bloom ever since, commemorating its own Silver Jubilee in 1999. Around forty of its fifty members can be found at each event, still held in the Village Hall each third Thursday. The club is affiliated to the National Association of Flower Arranging Societies and has raised substantial sums for charity. With coffee mornings and garden visits augmenting a monthly meeting calendar, the flower club shows no sign of wilting.

Children's Groups

September 1966 saw the first Brownie pack formed in the village. There had been an oversubscribed one in Bardsey for some time and this led to Ann Smith suggesting the village should have its own. Initial meetings were held at the Men's Institute and later,

One very successful group was the East Keswick Folk Dancing Team which was invited to perform at the Albert Hall before Princess Margaret. Our photo shows (left to right) Mr and Mrs Brian Hibbert, Mrs Susan Jackson, Mrs Freda Watson, Mrs Beryl Horry and Mr Ted Laughton

as numbers grew, at the Village Hall. In these early years, the group was linked to Bardsey but full independence came when it was registered in 1974.

The 1st East Keswick Guide Company was registered at Girl Guide Headquarters around the same time. A supporters' committee was established five years later and enthusiastic parents and friends have raised money ever since. Activities included an annual camp, jumble sales, litter collections, Christmas fairs and village galas. The guides held church parades in both the Anglican and Methodist churches, organised parties for senior citizens and helped to maintain Keswick Marsh. They regularly presented entertainments including the pantomime *Aladdin* in February 1982 which resulted in a substantial review in *Wetherby News*. In that article, East Keswick was described as 'a lively village and this is reflected in its guide company'. The first Queen's Guide in the unit was Jenny Phillips in 1979, later followed by Caroline Moscrop, Jenny Langford, Victoria Lupton, Sally Pease and Suzanne Avery. Nine years later, the first Baden Powell award was presented in the village hall to Julie Dalgleish. This was the highest award in the movement and seven more presentations quickly followed.

In 1987, the company amalgamated with the 1st Collingham who were unable to find a guider. This difficulty was resolved in 1994 so Collingham went its separate way again, however Bardsey amalgamated a year later for the same reason. 1999 saw a double commemoration marked by a grand reunion, the silver jubilee of the guide company and twentieth anniversary of its supporters' group.

A Rainbow Guide unit for 5 to 7 year olds was established at Easter 1996 attracting fifteen girls. That May, the whole pack were enrolled under a rainbow arch of helium-filled balloons which culminated in the release of the balloon arch carrying the girls' promises 'to do my best to love my God and to be kind and helpful' high above the village. If you add to this a Ranger Unit being demanded at the end of the millennium, the village potentially had activities for every girl and young woman from 5 to 14 years of age, and potentially to 25.

Young boys were not overlooked either. East Keswick Beavers opened in February 1994 with twelve boys aged six to eight from the village, Bardsey and Harewood. The aim of Beavers was to give young boys an introduction to scouting, and it met in the village hall on Tuesday evenings for an hour during term time. The group took part in annual St George's Day parades with Wetherby Scouts, contributed a stand to Beavers' Fun Days, took part in Beavers' Sports and had two meetings a year with Bardsey cubs, including an annual joint Halloween party.

It raised money and collected food parcels and toys for various refugee appeals including calling for outgrown underpants for Kosovo. Led by Julia Cockram and Janet Thornton the boys made mincemeat, cooked corn bread and pizzas, planted crocuses at the war memorial, undertook sponsored walks, made water-propelled rockets and balsa wood gliders.

In 1983, one of the village's most successful young persons' groups was established. The East Keswick Youth Club was designed to provide a meeting place and facilitate social events for young people between the ages of eight and fourteen. Meetings were held on Thursday evenings and split into two, with the younger half meeting at 6pm and the older half from 7.30pm.

The impetus for the group originally came from Leeds City Council who provided a subsidy. As well as the usual youth club activities, the group included sports, cinema visits, and trips to the bowling alley and climbing wall.

A large threat to the continuance of the group came in 1996 when Leeds decided to renovate and kit out a large black bus as a touring youth club. Instead of augmenting the youth club it was threatening to replace it. Many meetings followed and members lobbied public figures, councillors and the media and eventually the youth club's future was secured. The group relaunched with the acronym BEKS: Bardsey, East Keswick and Scarcroft. In the remaining years of the millennium it was attracting seventy young people a week with financial support from the Parish Council.

Countrywomen

Another hugely successful group is the East Keswick branch of the Yorkshire Countrywomen's Association. Formed in 1983, the group has a busy calendar of monthly meetings each first Tuesday, with guest speakers, rambles, walks, musical concerts, meals out and theatre trips.

Community Care

In March 1984, a meeting was called to examine whether the village could run a community care group. Those present agreed to seek the advice of the Voluntary Liaison Officer for Leeds Social Services and a successful village group was born. It quickly became renamed East Keswick Voluntary Care Group to emphasise that it was made up of volunteers and not connected to Social Services. It helped people of all ages who needed support and provided it in many ways from shopping for the elderly and collecting their pensions to simply visiting people living on their own who would welcome a chat. The group collected prescriptions, took people to hospital appointments, escorted the elderly to the village hairdresser and transported people to Good Companions in Bardsey and the Tuesday Club in East Keswick.

Badminton

The East Keswick Badminton Club was formed in April 1986 to provide those interested in the sport with playing and coaching opportunities at the Village Hall. Regular social activities were a part of its calendar including an Annual Dinner, a Christmas Party and a Barn Dance.

EsKape

A former vicar of Bardsey and East Keswick, the Reverend Russell, was instrumental in starting the village Young Wives group which was closely affiliated with the Mothers' Union of the Ripon Diocese. In the mid 1970s many young families had moved into new houses in the village and the group provided a good opportunity for them to meet each other. In 1990, the name became simply 'East Keswick Wives'. A recipe book complied by members raised over £800 for church funds, however falling attendance and worsening financial situation led to the group's disbandment in 1999. Out of this became EsKape, a group which formed in June 1999 with the sole aim of giving all women in the area an opportunity to socialise. In its first year the mixed programme included tennis, ten-pin bowling, guest speakers and treasure hunts.

Village Newsletter

The village has had its own newsletter for several decades. It began as an Anglican Church publication when East Keswick was part of the parish of Harewood. The eight-page publication was the local edition of one circulating over a much wider area where the centre four pages contained religious articles and the outer four pages specific local and mainly church news. When Canon Griffith died in 1974, East Keswick became part of the parish of Bardsey. The Vicar carried on the tradition but a new format including information provided by many secular groups in East Keswick was the result four years later. A member of the St Mary Magdalene congregation, Wendy Nutter, became editor in 1982 and the name of the publication became *Church & Village*. It was published monthly and distributed to every home in the village. In January 1999, the Parochial Church Council, which underwrote the cost of the publication, decided to amalgamate it with one they produced for Bardsey and which carried advertising and the new publication was to enjoy a combined circulation in excess of 1500 copies.

Church Groups

Churches Together in Bardsey and East Keswick is the name taken by an inter-church committee which coordinated and initiated ecumenical activity in the two villages from 1980 onwards. Originally known simply as the Inter-Church Committee, it changed its name after ten years to avoid confusion with a national organisation of a similar name. Representatives of the villages' four churches - St Mary Magdalene, East Keswick Methodist, the Church of the Blessed Sacrament and All Hallows - co-operated in the search for Christian unity. Worship, discussions and study groups formed the core of its activities coupled with occasional social events. The group had a significant part to play in the commemoration of the millennium in that it was involved in the local implementation of a national initiative to distribute a candle and millennium resolution to every home. The aim was to encourage all the population to share a moment of national reflection on the day chosen to mark the 2000th anniversary of Christ's birth.

None of the churches had a choir and this was the reason behind a group of singers from the two villages and Wike (which still had an Anglican church at the time) getting together the Ecumenical Choir from the late 1980s to provide a choir at special services and events. Its membership of fifteen rehearsed on Tuesday evenings at the Methodist Church and it was considered to be unique in its function. As years passed, the choir performed oratorios, music by modern composers, light concerts and sang with the Nidderdale Festival Choir for Choral Evensong at Pateley Bridge Church.

Soccer

The Football Club was formed in 1988 as the 'World's End' and played in the second division of the Harrogate Sunday League. Within two years it had won promotion to the first division and reached three cup semi-finals that year. In 1994 it changed its name to the East Keswick Football Club and played in Division Four of the Claro League.

A few years earlier it entered into an association with the Cricket Club which was being asked to vacate its Crabtree Lane ground at the time. The Football Club was playing from rented facilities in Knaresborough and it made sense to seek one joint set of facilities in the village. The East Keswick Sports Association was born, and found an eight-acre field at the junction of Moor Lane and Harewood Avenue which it was able to purchase from David Cooke with the help of grants from the Sports Council and the National Foundation for Sport and the Arts. A number of generous donations and fund raising made up the balance. The field was seeded and a pavilion built, enabling a number of social events to take place there. A covenant prevented a permanent bar on the site but occasional licences were allowed, and one of the most popular regular events taking place there was the annual village bonfire.

Toddler Groups

In the mid 1970s, a Mother and Toddler group became the forerunner to the East Keswick Playgroup which flourished in the village between 1979 and the 1990s. This group was to result in a further spin-off. Whilst mums with babies and toddlers were able to participate on the sidelines of the playgroup the situation was not ideal as the group was aimed at older children. Two village mums, Alison Booth and Lesley Benneworth, were the inspiration behind the East Keswick Toddler Group which started in June 1988. However the toddler group remained strongly linked to the playgroup, sharing many of its toys and much of its equipment.

The group was a registered charity run by volunteer mums and relied on fundraising activities including play days, jumble sales, teddy bear picnics and even a recipe book to supplement its income. Such was the appeal of the group that members came from surrounding villages.

Fresh Ideas

The village has never been short of ideas or enthusiastic people to implement them and even in the final year of the millennium there were new societies starting. Nan Hartley was involved in two. A Bridge Club was attracting interest as the millennium ended and a Short Mat Bowling Club had been started in February 1999. It had the aim of introducing a wide number of people to the sport. It was particularly appealing to retired people as it offered a means of exercise through the winter months and social interaction on three afternoons each week. Fifty members were involved; most transferring to play outdoor bowls at Bardsey during the summer.

15

The final night of a thousand years

Millennium Night, December 31st 1999, was to prove a fitting end to a thousand years. Some looked forward to it as the biggest excuse to party since VE day. Others thought it over-hyped and pointed out that celebrating two thousand years since the supposed birth of Christ was either four years too late or one year too early dependent upon which day you were working from. In the end, the churches decided to avoid arguments about the date and simply commemorate two thousand years of Christianity. The village representatives of Churches Together distributed a millennium candle and millennium prayer to every home. Part of a national initiative, the aim was to encourage each household to spend a few moments in quiet reflection on the true significance of the day and it is clear that many villagers did. Special services were held, some villagers particularly remarking upon the 'Welcome 2000' service in the Methodist Church at midday.

Some viewed the evening with trepidation. Doom mongers had warned of a millennium bug that might affect all manner of computerised equipment at midnight from traffic lights and air traffic control to automated bank machines and even the supply of power itself. Every organisation large and small spent vast sums to meet the threat of the millennium bug. In the event, nothing untoward happened.

For a while it looked as if the night might be a non-event. Many restaurants announced that far from partying, they were closing. They simply could not live up to the expectations associated with the high cost they would have to charge to cover staff wages. Nightclubs in Leeds had been advertising tickets at over-the-top prices, which

The village 1999

had fallen again and again as the night drew nearer and takers proved elusive. There was effectively no public transport apart from one night bus due to run on the A58 and taxis if they could be found… and afforded. The best solution for most was to stay put in the village and party with friends and neighbours.

In a poll especially conducted for this book, 38% of those who replied had celebrated outside the village, with the remainder either at home or elsewhere in East Keswick. Sixty per cent of people spent the evening in the company of friends, 23% at family gatherings and 17% quietly. No less than two thirds of those asked were at a party of some description. A quarter were at home, many watching worldwide celebrations unfold on TV, the remainder at a pub, working, or at church. A few were housebound by flu, which was worse that winter than for many years.

Some villagers celebrated further afield. A group of East Keswick friends went to Filey, a number of families went to London and even Antarctica was amongst locations which would be fondly remembered forever.

East Keswick celebrated the last day of the millennium in style. Several street parties were taking place throughout the village. In Keswick Grange, residents in evening dress set up a bar and disco in one double garage and turned a second into a restaurant where nineteen people sat down to a four-course meal, which included lobster as well as beef in red wine. In Church Drive, sixty adults and children were enjoying 'a night to remember forever'. A mild dry night was perfect for their fireworks. The village hall had been hired by the walking group whilst the football club on the outskirts of the village hosted a large party with midnight fireworks.

The Old Star Inn became ticket-only for the night. Eighty people paid £45 a head for an evening which included a lavish buffet, a half bottle of champagne per person, a bottle of wine and eight drinks of one's choice. The Duke of Wellington was one of relatively few pubs where all were welcome without paying an entry fee. Food was available to buy for those requiring it and the pub stayed open well into the night making use of relaxed licensing laws for the once-in-a-lifetime occasion.

As midnight struck, the whole of Britain seemed to erupt into a gigantic firework display. Even in the village, many residents were to comment on the fantastic display, which was not officially organised, simply the result of many simultaneous individual efforts creating pyrotechnics which would never be forgotten.

When asked in the millennium group questionnaire for views on the evening one villager wrote 'A great new year dinner party with 36 good friends. We felt very happy and lucky to be in East Keswick'. Another described it as 'a very enjoyable and special evening spent with our loved ones on the eve of the new millennium'. Others commented 'the fireworks were out of this world' and 'we are lucky to have great neighbours and friends with whom we wanted to share a special evening.' One couple probably spoke for many when they described an evening of drinks, food and fun; the millennium candle being lit at midnight, watching a tremendous aerial firework display and finally making it to bed at five in the morning.

As dawn broke on the first day of the new millennium the village was still very much a self-contained community with two pubs on Main Street and a third on Harewood Avenue, a post office/general store, well-respected butchers, two churches, and a village hall plus an evident community spirit and neighbourliness that only a minority of villages even come close to matching. Who were the people who made up this

The view from Blacksmith's Field 1999

community and what did they think of the issues affecting them? The questionnaire conducted for this chapter was not a scientific piece of market research, but nevertheless the results give a picture that might be interesting for future generations to look back on.

They were against foxhunting by the narrowest of margins, 40% to 39% with a fifth of those asked undecided. 60% felt the government did not understand the needs of the countryside. 11% thought they did, 29% had no opinion.

14% thought the monarchy irrelevant to the twenty-first century, 14% had no opinion but 72% disagreed with this proposition. 13% thought the Queen should abdicate in favour of Prince Charles, 64% disagreed and 23% were unsure.

15% thought our world had been visited by extra-terrestrial life. 50% disagreed and 35% had no opinion. Most people had an opinion on the reintroduction of the death penalty. 42% were in favour, 50% against.

24% thought Britain should withdraw from the European Community, 61% thought the UK should stay in and 15% had no opinion. However, only 16% were in favour of giving up sterling. 69% wanted to keep the pound and 15% had no opinion.

Only 9% of villagers read and followed their horoscopes. 73% did not believe in them and 18% were undecided.

The legalisation of soft drugs was favoured by 28% of the surveyed. 56% were against this and 16% had no opinion.

A significant proportion of the village had an email address and this book used a web site for research and book sales. 90% of respondents to the questionnaire believed the Internet was here to stay. A mere 1% disagreed. 9% were undecided.

56% described themselves as being computer literate, 36% were not and presumably the remaining 8% were in-between.

40% believed in life after death, 22% did not and 38% were unsure. 36% thought homosexuality ought to be covered at school, but 47% thought not and 17% were unsure. Finally 43% thought boxing ought to be banned, 31% disagreed and 25% were undecided.

East Keswick

We end our thousand year history with the names of the children who lived in our village at millennium dawn. As the sun touched the surrounding fields and woods that January morning, the future belonged to them. They were:

Alan Abram	(17/7/86)	James Nicolas George Burrell	(16/3/84)
Katie Abram	(13/6/88)	Harriet Burrell	(19/12/89)
Laura Abram	(28/10/92)		
Harry Abram	(22/3/94)	Alexa Louise Carter	(23/5/87)
Robert Mark Allison	(14/6/91)	Nathan Chomyszyn	(27/8/91)
Louise Clare Allison	(7/12/93)	Marcus Chomyszyn	(15/7/93)
		Alexi Chomyszyn	(7/8/96)
Charlotte Elizabeth Alport	(6/5/86)		
Poppy Elizabeth Alport	(18/10/90)	Matilda Hope Clough	(16/6/97)
Lauren Emma Baker	(26/11/98)	Esther Elizabeth Billie Cocker	(16/5/99)
Michael Ballman	(28/11/91)	Robert James Henry Cockram	(5/11/87)
Stefanie Ballman	(21/4/94)	Nicholas Alexander John Cockram	(3/10/89)
Matthew Jack Barstow	(26/2/99)	Ben Idrees Collins	(7/7/89)
		Yusaf Collins	(1/7/91)
Nichola Bassett	(12/2/86)	Mischa Sofie Collins	(23/12/94)
Cara Bassett	(28/4/88)		
		Edward Robert John Cooper	(15/7/86)
Grace Ella Bathurst	(6/7/99)		
		Ellie Jo Cowling	(21/10/98)
James Mark Batty	(8/10/95)		
Kathryn Ellen Batty	(17/4/97)	Caroline Elizabeth Dack	(1/4/91)
Joseph Andrew Batty	(19/6/99)	Christopher Henry John Dack	(31/3/93)
Thomas Andrew Beardsworth	(27/8/93)	Charles Davison	(16/9/98)
Alice Lucy Beardsworth	(6/6/95)		
Sophie Annabel Beardsworth	(7/2/98)	Kimberley Margaret Dee	(31/5/87)
		Nicholas Paul James Dee	(30/4/89)
Shane Ernest Bell	(21/9/91)		
		Matthew Doyle	(26/7/84)
Thomas Benneworth	(26/2/87)	Jessica Doyle	(2/5/87)
Lucy Benneworth	(23/5/90)		
		Jennifer Drake	(2/9/88)
Rachel Frances Bonney	(24/5/92)	Caroline Drake	(14/9/90)
Emily Victoria Bonney	(20/1/96)		
Charlotte Eloise Bonney	(23/11/99)	John Thomas Eaton	(25/2/99)

Angus Erskine	(18/1/96)	James Edward Jackson	(7/10/83)
Archie Erskine	(12/1/98)	Harriet Jackson	(20/4/86)
Tony Evans	(24/7/90)	Emma Louise Johnston	(24/11/86)
Gareth Evans	(24/2/92)	Catherine Alice Johnston	(26/10/88)
		Michael Peter Robert Johnston	(10/6/92)
Georgina Barbara Fletcher	(12/3/95)		
		Samuel Michael Joy	(14/8/99)
Lisa Irene Galinsky	(2/9/91)	Emily Jane Kerr	(23/12/85)
Edwin John Dickson Gardiner	(8/10/87)	Louisa Kitchingman	(11/8/84)
Charlotte Emily Helen Sylvia Gardiner		Sarah Kitchingman	(27/5/86)
	(29/12/88)	Edward Kitchingman	(1/5/90)
Tristan Phillip Gibbs	(29/4/87)	David Michael Lifford	(18/5/84)
Harriet Olivia Gibbs	(3/9/92)	Michael Mason Lifford	(24/3/86)
Stephen Lance Greenwood	(6/2/91)	Sophie Elizabeth Lord	(1/9/87)
Robert Carl Greenwood	(26/2/94)	Edward Jeremy Lord	(30/4/90)
James Paul Greenwood	(27/3/96)	Alexander David Lord	(21/5/92)
James Alan Guildford	(23/8/84)	Gareth McGreavy	(23/5/87)
		Georgina McGreavy-Dowd	(12/11/94)
Harry Hamburg	(13/8/85)		
Sarah Hamburg	(6/11/86)	Charlotte Elizabeth Mackie	(19/10/98)
Imogen Margaret Grace Hammond	(14/5/99)	Saimon Oliver Mills	(4/7/92)
		Jenny Kumari Mills	(21/10/94)
Emma Hartley	(4/5/90)		
James Hartley	(27/2/92)	Charlotte Rebbeca Alice Milner	(16/9/87)
Thomas Hartley	(24/1/96)	Joseph Alexander Nicholson Milner	(14/6/91)
William Hartley	(24/12/98)	Daniel George Louis Milner	(1/9/92)
Oliver George Hinchliffe	(30/5/84)	Rowland Paul Moseley	(30/7/83)
		Heather Charlotte Moseley	(24/2/86)
Victoria Hurcomb	(31/3/89)		
Abbey Hurcomb	(31/1/92)	Oliver John Myers	(24/5/96)
		Melissa Anne Myers	(26/11/98)
Melise Icel	(15/2/99)		

East Keswick

Rebecca Elizabeth Normington	(14/12/87)	Thomas James Smith	(11/9/99)
Sean Martin Normington	(15/8/89)		
Philipa Rae Normington	(24/1/96)	Jacob Harvey Stanley	(17/7/94)
		Rachel Hannah Victoria Stanley	(7/10/98)
Alexandra Thea Payne	(30/11/90)	William David Michael Stanley	(19/11/99)
Samantha Peace	(26/1/83)	Katy Stocks	(1/5/83)
Angela Peace	(14/5/85)	Charlotte Stocks	(13/5/84)
		Emily Stocks	(23/3/87)
David Steven Pierce	(30/8/93)		
Sara Louise Pierce	(11/10/97)	Alice Mary Thornton	(31/3/89)
		Emma Rose Thornton	(8/4/91)
Siobhan Eleanor Place	(7/12/96)		
		Maximilian Toone	(23/6/95)
Samuel Max Port	(28/1/92)	Emmanuelle Toone	(14/9/96)
Saskia Lena Port	(14/2/94)	Chiara Toone	(20/8/99)
Yardena Maya Port	(18/3/96)		
Inbal Hannah Port	(8/10/99)	Caitlin Ward	(8/12/97)
Ian Rankin	(12/5/93)	Louise Sinead Waterfield	(30/11/90)
Frances Rankin	(19/12/94)	Adam Patrick Waterfield	(28/12/93)
		Dominic Sean Waterfield	(19/6/98)
Megan Alexandra Reid	(23/1/93)		
Elliott George Reid	(2/7/95)	Michael Watson	(14/7/87)
Gabriella Lucy Reid	(7/12/99)	James Watson	(21/3/90)
		Oliver Joseph Watson	(5/11/97)
Jack William Render	(19/10/97)		
		Richard Samuel Watts	(26/4/84)
Anna Mary Renfree	(10/5/83)		
		Kate Sarah Edith Whiteley	(10/3/91)
Helen Laura Searle	(8/11/90)	Jonathan Frederick Whiteley	(18/2/94)
Bryn Scholey	(31/3/87)	Sophie Jane Wilkinson	(15/10/85)
		Richard Michael Wilkinson	(28/1/88)
Andrew Sharp	(7/9/85)		
		Hattie Wood	(21/9/89)
Matthew David Siekierkowski	(16/4/87)		
Joseph George Siekierkowski	(24/6/90)	Lauren Jane Wright	(26/2/89)
Dominic Philip Siekierkowski	(12/2/93)	Bethan Ceri Wright	(27/2/92)
Sarah Emma Smalley	(15/8/98)		
Richard Smith	(15/4/85)	Adam Young	(5/3/95)
Robert Smith	(2/6/87)	Nyree Keisha Young	(14/2/96)